The Moon

The Moon's phases have long influenced gardeners. The new and first-quarter phases are good for planting above-ground crops, putting down turf, grafting trees and transplanting. From the full moon through to the last quarter is the best time for killing weeds, pruning, mowing and planting below-ground crops.

right around the Earth. However, as the Earth is also moving the Moon has to travel a bit further to get back to its starting position and it takes 29.5 days to travel right around the Earth. This is called a lunar month.

A new moon, sometimes known as the dark moon, is the beginning of the lunar cycle. It occurs when the Earth, the Moon and the Sun are in perfect alignment. Each new moon appears dark to us because the Sun is illuminating the side of the Moon that we cannot see and it gets lost in the glare of the Sun. It is a time of rest and renewal and is an ideal time to implement new plans and begin new projects.

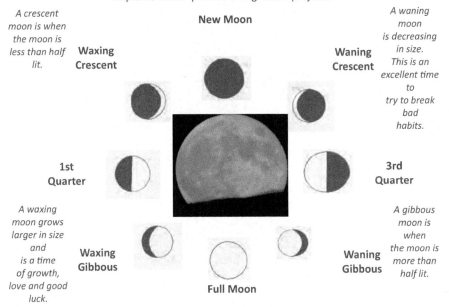

A crescent moon is when the moon is less than half lit.

New Moon

A waning moon is decreasing in size. This is an excellent time to try to break bad habits.

Waxing Crescent

Waning Crescent

1st Quarter

3rd Quarter

A waxing moon grows larger in size and is a time of growth, love and good luck.

Waxing Gibbous

Waning Gibbous

A gibbous moon is when the moon is more than half lit.

Full Moon

During 2024 we will see two super full moons on 18th September and 17th October. A super full moon is when a full moon takes place at its closest approach to Earth. We have a true Blue Moon on 19th August, ie the third full moon in a season with four full moons – It is a common misconception that a Blue Moon is a second moon in a calendar month. Another lunar event this year is a partial lunar eclipse on 18th September which, as mentioned earlier, will be during a super full moon. We have used the names in accordance with the Old English tradition and the astronomical information is set for London, England, and has been adjusted for daylight-saving time.

Calendar Customs

January – is a good time to be optimistic about the year ahead. If good luck is forth-coming on the 1st, it will continue throughout the year. Twelfth Night marks the end of festivities, with Distaff Day and Plough Monday marking the start of work.

February – begins with Imbolc, half-way between the Winter Solstice and the Spring Equinox, when the first signs of spring begin to emerge.

March – starts with St. David's Day, the patron saint of Wales, then on the 17th Ireland's St. Patrick is remembered. The third week of March sees the Spring Equinox, followed shortly by the change to British Summer Time when we start to see a real difference in our daylight hours.

April – always begins with All Fools' Day, and then on the 23rd England's St. George is remembered. Easter can fall anywhere between 22nd March and 25th April, depending on when the full moon after 21st March occurs.

May – brings us May Day with all its associated celebrations from maypoles to morris dancing. This truly is the time to look forward to the summer ahead.

June – is a month that is full of fairs, and with the summer equinox falling in the third week, which is one of the most significant days in the ancient calendar.

August – begins with Lammas/Lughnasadh; for Christians it is Loaf-Mass Day, when bread made from the new wheat crop was blessed. For the Celts, Gaels and more recently Neo-pagans it is a time to celebrate the new harvest.

July – continues with fairs and wakes, with the prospect of rain. If it rains on the 15th St. Swithun's Day, it is believed that rain will follow for forty days!

September - the Autumn harvest is now in full swing as farmers gather their crops before the weather turns. Michael-mas Day on the 29th was a time for rent collection and the hiring of staff, as well as the last day to pick blackberries 'before the Devil spoiled them'.

October – was a time for goose fairs, of which Nottingham and Tavistock fairs still survive. The month ends with Samhain / All Hallows' Eve, when the veil between our world and the next is at its thinnest!

November – begins with Hallantide, encompassing All Saints' Day (1st) and All Souls' Day (2nd). Souling took place on these days when men and boys would perform souling songs in return for 'a dole of soul cakes'. Bonfires were traditionally lit, which were eventually supplanted by Guy Fawkes bonfires.

December – seems to be taken up entirely with Yuletide traditions, starting on St. Nicholas's Day on the 6th. With the Winter Solstice on or around the 21st, it has always been an important time for celebration.

Welcome to our diary, a journey through the year that we can take together. If we listen to, and live attuned to, the natural rhythms of nature, then our lives will be far less stressful than if we constantly seem to 'fight against the tide'. Our annual cycle of traveling around the sun gives us solstices and equinoxes and seasons. The solstices are when time itself appears still and for a few days our sun appears stationary, either giving us limited or plentiful daylight. We too can pause at these points and take the time to reflect on the changing seasons and observe nature at her most abundant or most empty. The equinoxes are a time of balance, and we too can react to this in our lives, addressing things that may have taken over more than we would wish. Balance brings back a more sustainable and harmonious way of living. We can also pledge to bring balance and sustainability to our environment too and give more time to noticing nature at these very wonderful times of the year.

Monday 1

Sunrise 08.06
Sunset 16.01
Moonset 11.06
Moonrise 21.52

New Year's Day

Tuesday 2

Sunrise 08.06
Sunset 16.02
Moonset 11.17
Moonrise 23.02

Wednesday 3

Sunrise 08.05
Sunset 16.03
Moonset 11.26
Moonrise -- --

Thursday 4

Sunrise 08.05
Sunset 16.04
Moonrise 00.11
Moonset 11.36

Third Quarter 03.30

Friday 5

Sunrise 08.05
Sunset 16.06
Moonrise 01.23
Moonset 11.48

Twelfth Night

Saturday 6

Sunrise 08.05
Sunset 16.07
Moonrise 02.38
Moonset 12.02

Epiphany

Sunday 7

Sunrise 08.04
Sunset 16.08
Moonrise 03.57
Moonset 12.20

Distaff Day

The First Week of January

"Blow out the old, Blow in the new, Blow out the false And blow in the true." This rhyme was meant to be sung as midnight rang in by someone stepping outside and then returning indoors to wish everyone a 'Happy New Year'.

Weather conditions during the first three days of the year were meant to indicate the kind of weather people could expect in the following three months. This belief was later applied to the first twelve days, resulting in a long range weather forecast for the following twelve months.Wassailing takes place from the days leading up to Christmas, during the twelve days of Christmas and through to old Twelfth Night on the 16th January. To wake up the apple trees and scare off harmful sprites people sing traditional wassail songs, bang pans and even fire guns!

Depending on whether the Twelve Days of Christmas are counted from Christmas Day or Boxing Day, Twelfth Night falls on either the 5th or the 6th January . In Ireland, particularly in Kerry and Cork, January 6th, The Feast of the Epiphany, is also known as Nollaig na mBan, meaning "Women's Christmas". On this day, the menfolk stay at home and women go out for a meal and a drink to pamper themselves after their hard work over the festive season. According to a joke in The Irish Times; "even God rested on the seventh day; Irish women didn't stop until the twelfth!"

In Victorian times, Epiphany Tarts – ornately decorated plate-sized jam tarts - were made. Baking competitions at church suppers were fiercely contested, although tarts featuring the most complicated design and generous amounts of jam usually took first prize. Traditionally Christmas decorations are taken down to avoid bad luck as Christmastide concludes.

Monday 8

Sunrise 08.04
Sunset 16.09
Moonrise 05.19
Moonset 12.47

Plough Monday

Tuesday 9

Sunrise 08.03
Sunset 16.11
Moonrise 06.40
Moonset 13.27

Wednesday 10

Sunrise 08.03
Sunset 16.12
Moonrise 07.50
Moonset 14.26

Thursday 11

Sunrise 08.02
Sunset 16.14
Moonrise 08.44
Moonset 15.45

New Moon 11.57

Friday 12

Sunrise 08.02
Sunset 16.15
Moonrise 09.22
Moonset 17.16

Saturday 13

Sunrise 08.01
Sunset 16.16
Moonrise 09.48
Moonset 18.50

Sunday 14

Sunrise 08.00
Sunset 16.18
Moonrise 10.06
Moonset 20.22

January is a time for both slumber and awakening. A redoubtable winter sleeper is the dormouse, whose name originates from the French word 'dormir', meaning 'to sleep'. This little creature sleeps from September until April and slows its metabolism down by 90 per cent to conserve energy. During this time snowdrops and catkins emerge, bringing hope and joy in wintertime.

January

Winter

Monday 15

Sunrise 07.59
Sunset 16.20
Moonrise 10.21
Moonset 21.50

Tuesday 16

Sunrise 07.59
Sunset 16.21
Moonrise 10.34
Moonset 23.15

Wednesday 17

Sunrise 07.58
Sunset 16.23
Moonrise 10.47
Moonset -- --

Thursday 18

Sunrise 07.57
Sunset 16.24
Moonset 00.39
Moonrise 11.00

First Quarter 03.52

Friday 19

Sunrise 07.56
Sunset 16.26
Moonset 02.03
Moonrise 11.17

Saturday 20

Sunrise 07.55
Sunset 16.28
Moonset 03.27
Moonrise 11.38

Sunday 21

Sunrise 07.54
Sunset 16.29
Moonset 04.48
Moonrise 12.07

St. Agnes Day

The Witch's Heart

In the Tuesday Market Place in Kings Lynn, the mark of the Witch's Heart can be seen in the brickwork above a window of a townhouse. This crudely carved heart in a diamond shape is associated with the tale of Margaret Read, 1590, who was said to have been burned as a witch. There is little known about this event other than an entry in "The History of Antiquities of the Flourishing Corporation of Kings Lynn", published by Benjamin Mackerell in 1738. Although some people doubt its authenticity, an enduring legend remains of Margaret's heart bursting from her body as she was burned in the market square, then striking the brickwork, leaving it marked with the 'heart' that can still be seen today. Then, with an energy all of its own, the heart is said to have bounced its way to the river, causing the water to froth and boil.

As to whether Margaret existed, there is indeed a record of a child being baptised Margaret Read on 25th March 1568, the daughter of William and Joane Read, making Margaret 22 at the time of her death. Alternatively, there is Margrett Hammond, who married Thomas Read at St Margaret's Church in Kings Lynn on 8th April 1562. There is no record of either woman's death.

There are other tales associated with innocent women being wrongly condemned and the Witch's Heart carving. One such tale is about a housemaid who was to inherit her mistress's fortune when she died. On hearing this the maid's lover proposed to her, a will was written, and the maid's mistress was murdered. The maid was arrested and burnt at the stake. It is said she shouted that her innocent heart would burst from her chest, which it did, and so marked the wall that it hit as a reminder of her innocence.

Another local story associated with the general fear of evil pervading this area is recorded in the local church.

"It is said that the Devil's hoof print is to be seen in Devil's Alley, off Nelson Street in Kings Lynn. The Devil arrived by ship to the town and disembarked to steal some souls, but he was spotted by a priest who drove him away with prayers and a dousing with holy water. The infuriated Devil stamped his hoof so hard that he left his imprint."

Monday 22

Sunrise 07.52
Sunset 16.31
Moonset 06.01
Moonrise 12.47

Tuesday 23

Sunrise 07.51
Sunset 16.33
Moonset 07.02
Moonrise 13.40

Wednesday 24

Sunrise 07.50
Sunset 16.34
Moonset 07.48
Moonrise 14.46

Thursday 25

Sunrise 17.49
Sunset 16.36
Moonset 08.20
Moonrise 15.59

'Old Moon' 17.54 / Burns Night

Friday 26

Sunrise 07.48
Sunset 16.38
Moonset 08.43
Moonrise 17.14

Saturday 27

Sunrise 07.46
Sunset 16.40
Moonset 09.00
Moonrise 18.27

Sunday 28

Sunrise 07.45
Sunset 16.41
Moonset 09.13
Moonrise 19.39

The Blackbird

The nightingale has a lyre of gold,
The lark's is a clarion-call,
And the blackbird plays but a boxwood flute,
But I love him best of all.

For his song is all of the joy of life,
And we in the mad, spring weather,
We two have listened till he sang
Our hearts and lips together.

William Ernest Henley 19th century

The Blackbird was often known as an Ouzel and in Shakespeare's 'A Midsummers Night's Dream' Bottom speaks of *"the ouzel cock so black of hue, with orange tawny bill"*. The name Blackbird was certainly known by the 17th century, but both names persisted for many years.

In County Meath, it is said that *"when the Blackbird sings before Christmas, she will cry before Candlemas".* This could refer to the early nesting cycle of the Blackbird, which can get caught out in severe winters when it nests too early, thus making their chicks vulnerable to the cold, although the adults are quite robust when it comes to surviving harsh weather.

St. Kevin was said to have had a Blackbird lay her eggs in the palm of his hand, and he remained with his arm outstretched aloft until the brood had hatched and then fledged.

Monday 29
Sunrise 07.44
Sunset 16.43
Moonset 09.24
Moonrise 20.49

Tuesday 30
Sunrise 07.42
Sunset 16.45
Moonset 09.33
Moonrise 21.58

Wednesday 31
Sunrise 07.41
Sunset 16.47
Moonset 09.43
Moonrise 23.08

Thursday 1
Sunrise 07.39
Sunset 16.48
Moonset 09.53
Moonrise -- --

Imbolc / St. Bridgid's Day

Friday 2
Sunrise 07.38
Sunset 16.50
Moonrise 00.20
Moonset 10.06

Third Quarter 23.18 / Candlemas

Saturday 3
Sunrise 07.36
Sunset 16.52
Moonrise 01.36
Moonset 10.21

Sunday 4
Sunrise 07.34
Sunset 16.54
Moonrise 02.55
Moonset 10.43

Imbolc

February 1st, also known as Imbolc, was, and still feels like, an auspicious day as we leave the long month of January behind and feel a change in the air. In Scotland, people would look to the skies and shores for the arrival of Oystercatchers who heralded the arrival of spring, as did adders emerging from their nests and badgers coming out of their dens on the following day, Candlemas. It was thought that if badgers did not emerge on that day then winter would continue.
This could be the origin of Groundhog Day in America, where Punxsutawney Phil, a groundhog, is watched by crowds of people to see if he comes out of his den, at Gobblers Knob in Pennsylvania, and sees his hadow, thus signalling no end to winter just yet.

The earliest mentions of Imbolc are in Irish literature from the 10th century and appears to align the day with the birthing cycle of ewe's. The day is 'shared' with the Celtic Goddess Bridgid, who became know as a saint with the acceptance of Christianity, and who has her feast day on this day.

Last year a three-year campaign by Herstory resulted in a new national holiday in Ireland to honour her as matron saint, Celtic goddess, role model for our times and protector of nature, animals and all living things.
It was traditional to hang a 'Bridgid's Cross' made of rushes above the door each year, then the old cross would be burnt or hidden in the roof.

Imbolc is a time for possibilities, hope, adversity, anticipation and the need for a little patience, as we wait for winter to complete its cycle and look forward to the ever-welcome first signs of spring.

Monday 5
Sunrise 07.33
Sunset 16.56
Moonrise 04.15
Moonset 11.15

Tuesday 6
Sunrise 07.31
Sunset 16.58
Moonrise 05.29
Moonset 12.04

Wednesday 7
Sunrise 07.29
Sunset 16.59
Moonrise 06.31
Moonset 13.12

Thursday 8
Sunrise 07.28
Sunset 17.01
Moonrise 07.16
Moonset 14.38

Friday 9
Sunrise 07.26
Sunset 17.03
Moonrise 07.47
Moonset 16.13

New Moon 22.59

Saturday 10
Sunrise 07.24
Sunset 17.05
Moonrise 08.09
Moonset 17.49

Sunday 11
Sunrise 07.22
Sunset 17.07
Moonrise 08.25
Moonset 19.22

You can make a heart out of tissue paper filled with seeds to give to someone as a symbol of love and new beginnings.

Oystercatchers were known as 'Gille Brighde' in Ireland, meaning 'the servants of Bride'. This was because they make their appearance at the time of Bridgid's Day/Imbolc at the start of February, bringing spring with them.

Monday 12

Sunrise 07.21
Sunset 17.09
Moonrise 08.39
Moonset 20.52

Tuesday 13

Sunrise 07.19
Sunset 17.10
Moonrise 08.52
Moonset 22.20

Shrove Tuesday

Wednesday 14

Sunrise 07.17
Sunset 17.12
Moonrise 09.06
Moonset 23.47

Valentine's Day

Thursday 15

Sunrise 07.15
Sunset 17.14
Moonrise 09.21
Moonset -- --

Friday 16

Sunrise 07.13
Sunset 17.16
Moonset 01.14
Moonrise 09.41

First Quarter 15.00

Saturday 17

Sunrise 07.11
Sunset 17.18
Moonset 02.38
Moonrise 10.07

Sunday 18

Sunrise 07.09
Sunset 17.20
Moonset 03.54
Moonrise 10.44

Plant Beans Day

In Berkeley Vale, Gloucestershire, a rhyme dating from at least 1620, *"On St Valentine's Day, Cast beans in clay"*, suggests gardening, rather than love, was on people's minds.

However, in Roy Palmer's Book, "The Folklore of Gloucestershire", a Miss A Smith, of Great Rissington, is recorded as remembering this rhyme being used by children begging from door to door on Valentine's Day,

"Good Morrow to you, Valentine,
I'll be yours if you'll be mine.
Give us a penny and save us all.
One for Peter and one for Paul,
And one for the little boy over the wall."

Valentine Dealing, a Victorian custom, was a sure-fire way of having a Valentine for at least a year. An equal number of male and female names were written on pieces of paper and put into separate hats. The hats were passed round the group taking part and a name was selected from the appropriate hat. The paired couples then exchanged gifts and became sweethearts for that year.

In Somerset, people who didn't have any Valentines were called Dusters. Sadly, those who did get Valentines enjoyed teasing the Dusters by pretending to sweep them up with brushes and other cleaning items.

"Roses are red, Violets are blue,
Carnations are sweet and so are you.
And so are they that send you this,
And when we meet, we'll have a kiss."
A children's Valentine rhyme

Love Divination:

Place a sprig of Thyme in one shoe and a sprig of Rosemary in the other, sprinkle with water three times, place under your bed to dream of whom you'll future wed.

Monday 19
Sunrise 07.07
Sunset 17.21
Moonset 04.59
Moonrise 11.34

Tuesday 20
Sunrise 07.05
Sunset 17.23
Moonset 05.49
Moonrise 12.36

Wednesday 21
Sunrise 07.03
Sunset 17.25
Moonset 06.24
Moonrise 13.47

Thursday 22
Sunrise 07.01
Sunset 17.27
Moonset 06.49
Moonrise 15.01

Friday 23
Sunrise 06.59
Sunset 17.29
Moonset 07.07
Moonrise 16.15

Saturday 24
Sunrise 06.57
Sunset 17.30
Moonset 07.21
Moonrise 17.27

'Snow Moon' 12.30

Sunday 25
Sunrise 06.55
Sunset 17.32
Moonset 07.32
Moonrise 18.38

Nickanan Night

Nickanan Night, also known as Roguery Night or Peasen Monday, is a Cornish feast traditionally held on the Monday before Shrove Tuesday. It once held great significance in Cornwall and was primarily a time to eat pea soup, which was prepared in most homes in the county using split peas. However, for children and youths it was a time for mischief. This involved knocking on doors and then running away before being caught, or demanding a pancake to avoid further trouble for the household. Often items were taken from the property only to be found the next day displayed around the village.

In some places, such as Polperro, an effigy representing Judas Iscariot, called a 'Jack-o-Lent', was paraded through the streets and pelted with rotten vegetables. It was then taken to the beach where it was ceremonially burned.

Thomas Quiller-Couch, a 19th-century naturalist, recorded this description of the night's events;

"On the day, about the dusk of the evening, it is the custom for boys to prowl about the streets with short clubs, and to knock loudly at every door, running off to escape detection. If, however, no attention be excited, and especially if any article be carelessly guarded, then the things are carried away; and on the following day are discovered displayed in some conspicuous place. The time when this is practised is called 'Nicka-nan night' and the individuals concerned are supposed to represent some imps of darkness, that seize on and expose unguarded moments."

A rhyme would be recited by the youngsters to accompany the night's merriment.

"Nicka nicka nan
Give me some pancake, and then I'll be gone
But if you give me none
I'll throw a great stone
And down your door shall come."

Monday 26
Sunrise 06.53
Sunset 17.34
Moonset 07.42
Moonrise 19.47

Tuesday 27
Sunrise 06.51
Sunset 17.36
Moonset 07.51
Moonrise 20.57

Wednesday 28
Sunrise 06.49
Sunset 17.38
Moonset 08.01
Moonrise 22.08

Thursday 29
Sunrise 06.46
Sunset 17.39
Moonset 08.12
Moonrise 23.22

Friday 1
Sunrise 06.44
Sunset 17.41
Moonset 08.26
Moonrise -- --

St. David's Day (Patron Saint of Wales)

Saturday 2
Sunrise 06.42
Sunset 17.43
Moonrise 00.38
Moonset 08.45

Sunday 3
Sunrise 06.40
Sunset 17.45
Moonrise 01.57
Moonset 09.11

Third Quarter 15.23

"There are fairies at the bottom of our garden."

In 1917, the same year that children's poet Rose Fyleman published her poem, 'Fairies', two cousins, Elsie Wright aged 16 and Frances Griffiths aged nine, took some photographs of fairies in Cottingley Beck, which flowed behind Elsie's home. Frances, who had been living in South Africa, was staying with the Wright family at their home in Cottingley, West Yorkshire.

The fairy photos intrigued those people who were inclined to believe in these supernatural beings right up until the 1980s, when Geoffrey Crawley, the editor of the "British Journal of Photography", undertook a major investigation and concluded they were fakes. The most eminent believer in the fairies was Sir Arthur Conan Doyle, who was made aware of them through his involvement in the Theosophical Society, to whom Elsie's mother had taken the photos.

In 1983 Elsie, as an elderly lady, confessed that the photos were fake, but Frances insisted all her life that the fifth and last photo, 'Fairies and their Sunbath', was real.
Elsie's father, Arthur, was an amateur photographer with his own darkroom and had the equipment Elsie needed to develop the photographic plates. Elsie was a keen amateur photographer and had experience in retouching photographs. Her father always suspected that the images were fake.
The fairies were eventually discovered to be drawings copied from images in "Princess Mary's Gift Book", published in 1914, which had had wings added to them. They were then propped up and photographed by the girls.

Monday 4

Sunrise 06.38
Sunset 17.46
Moonrise 03.12
Moonset 09.51

Tuesday 5

Sunrise 06.36
Sunset 17.48
Moonrise 04.18
Moonset 10.48

St. Piran's Day

Wednesday 6

Sunrise 06.33
Sunset 17.50
Moonrise 05.09
Moonset 12.04

Thursday 7

Sunrise 06.31
Sunset 17.52
Moonrise 05.45
Moonset 13.33

Friday 8

Sunrise 06.29
Sunset 17.53
Moonrise 06.10
Moonset 15.08

Saturday 9

Sunrise 06.27
Sunset 17.55
Moonrise 06.29
Moonset 16.43

Sunday 10

Sunrise 06.24
Sunset 17.57
Moonrise 06.44
Moonset 18.16

New Moon 09.00 / Mothering Sunday

Starlings

Nature Note

Starlings get their name from the Old English word 'Staer', which may mean 'spotted' or 'flecked' and allude to their plumage, which is best seen during autumn and winter. During this time Starlings congregate in huge flocks before roosting and perform breathtaking acrobatics, called murmurations, before descending to their roost site.

Mythology

Starlings are related to Myna birds and, as such, can be taught to speak. A medieval Welsh story tells of Branwen, the daughter of Llyr. When she was mistreated by her Irish husband, Branwen taught a tame Starling to speak and sent him home across the Irish Sea to inform her brother Bran, who mustered an army to rescue her.

Old Names

Some old names for the Starling areSheep Stare (Somerset) - due to its habit of alighting on the backs of sheep to pick at the ticks in their coats. Other names include Starn (Shetland), Starnal (Northampton), Sheppie (Cheshire) and Black Felt (North Riding).

Monday 11

Sunrise 06.22
Sunset 17.58
Moonrise 06.57
Moonset 19.48

Tuesday 12

Sunrise 06.20
Sunset 18.00
Moonrise 07.10
Moonset 21.19

Wednesday 13

Sunrise 06.19
Sunset 18.02
Moonrise 07.25
Moonset 22.49

Thursday 14

Sunrise 06.15
Sunset 18.04
Moonrise 07.43
Moonset -- --

Friday 15

Sunrise 06.13
Sunset 18.05
Moonset 00.18
Moonrise 08.07

Saturday 16

Sunrise 06.11
Sunset 18.07
Moonset 01.41
Moonrise 08.41

Sunday 17

Sunrise 06.09
Sunset 18.09
Moonset 02.53
Moonrise 09.27

First Quarter 04.10 / St. Patrick's Day (Patron Saint of Ireland)

As the daylight hours are increasing, woodlands are coming to life and hedgehogs are emerging from hibernation. Birds are nest building and can be seen flitting around hedgerows with moss, twigs and threads of fleece in their beaks.

The Cowslip is just beginning to flower, believed to be so named because it is supposed to spring up where a patch of cow-dung has fallen. The odour of the Cowslip is said to calm the heart. In Kent they are known as 'Fairy Cups'.

Monday 18

Sunrise 06.06
Sunset 18.10
Moonset 03.48
Moonrise 10.26

Tuesday 19

Sunrise 06.04
Sunset 18.12
Moonset 04.28
Moonrise 11.35

Wednesday 20

Sunrise 06.02
Sunset 18.14
Moonset 04.55
Moonrise12.49

Ostara / Vernal / Spring Equinox 03.07 / Spring officially begins

Thursday 21

Sunrise 06.00
Sunset 18.16
Moonset 05.15
Moonrise 14.03

Friday 22

Sunrise 05.57
Sunset 18.17
Moonset 05.30
Moonrise 15.16

Saturday 23

Sunrise 05.55
Sunset 18.19
Moonset 05.41
Moonrise 16.27

Sunday 24

Sunrise 05.53
Sunset 18.21
Moonset 05.51
Moonrise 17.37

Vernal Equinox - Comings and Goings

This is a time of comings and goings as birds, such as the Whooper Swan, are now making ready to leave our shores, having overwintered here to return to their summer residences in Euro-Siberia. We can now look to the skies for the return of early Martins, and Swallows returning from Africa, while waiting eagerly to hear the call of the first Cuckoo. Already our resident birds are getting more animated and the distinctive song of the Yellowhammer - "A little bit of bread and cheese pleeese" - is beginning to fill the air.

Blackthorn blossom brings a froth of white, that almost looks like snowfall, to the roadside verges and hedgerows. This plant is often associated with witches, the darker half of the year and winter, yet it is one of the first indicators of true spring, together with Forsythia and other early-flowering trees and shrubs. The Hawthorn has leaf buds ready to burst, unlike the Blackthorn, which gives us its blossom before its leaves.

This new spring energy can be put to use by doing some spring cleaning in your life and in your home. Taking stock of what needs to be kept and what needs to go can have a very positive impact as we de-clutter and keep what we most need and cherish. Simplifying and streamlining our lives and our homes can be restorative and will also benefit others, as we can give things away to those who have a better use for them. If this feels like a step too far, then maybe just go for a good old house cleaning session, throwing open the doors and windows to let the remnants of winter out and welcome springtime into your home.

Intentions; Balance, energy, emergence.
Actions; Planting seeds (actual and metaphorical), spring cleaning, being in nature.
Foods; Spring greens, eggs, asparagus.
Springtime Saying; *"If you see the cuckoo sitting, The swallow flitting, And a filly foal lying still, You all the year shall have your will."*
Burne, Shropshire 1883

Monday 25

Sunrise 05.50
Sunset 18.22
Moonset 06.01
Moonrise 18.46

'Lenten' Moon 07.00 / Lady Day (Quarter Day)

Tuesday 26

Sunrise 05.48
Sunset 18.24
Moonset 06.10
Moonrise 19.57

Wednesday 27

Sunrise 05.46
Sunset 18.26
Moonset 06.21
Moonrise 21.11

Thursday 28

Sunrise 05.44
Sunset 18.27
Moonset 06.34
Moonrise 22.27

Maundy Thursday

Friday 29

Sunrise 05.41
Sunset 18.29
Moonset 06.50
Moonrise 23.44

Good Friday

Saturday 30

Sunrise 05.39
Sunset 18.31
Moonset 07.13
Moonrise -- --

Put the clocks forward one hour at bedtime

Sunday 31

Sunrise 06.37
Sunset 19.32
Moonrise 02.01
Moonset 08.47

Easter Sunday / British Summer Time begins

Easter

Not everything about Easter is associated with eggs, bunnies and chocolate. Eastertide attracts many unusual customs, traditions and sayings. For example, if you want good fortune at Easter, then you need a new outfit!

"Every person must have some part at least of his dress new on Easter Sunday, or he will have no good fortune that year."
1830, Forby East Anglia.

"Now Easter holidays draw near, for maids their best new gowns to wear."
circa 1735.

"Donkeys kneel at the moment of sunrise on Easter morning, and they bray three times at sunrise on Good Friday."
Northern Ireland

Divination also plays its part at this time of year.

"If anyone looks into St. Austin's Well, in Cerne Abbas, first thing on Easter morning, he will see the faces of those who will die within the year."
Dorset 1899

The Sunday after Easter marked the beginning of Hocktide. Hock Sunday was known by some as "Quasimodo Sunday" as the traditional beginning to the church service on this day was *"Quasi modo geniti infantes"* (trans.- as if newborn babies).

Another name for this day was Balaam's Ass Day, originating from the Bible story which was traditionally read at services on this day.

There is also a saying that *"Mackerel come into season when Balaam's Ass speaks to the church!"*

Monday 1

Sunrise 06.34
Sunset 19.34
Moonrise 03.09
Moonset 09.36

Easter Monday / All Fools' Day

Tuesday 2

Sunrise 06.32
Sunset 19.36
Moonrise 04.04
Moonset 10.43

Third Quarter 04.14

Wednesday 3

Sunrise 06.30
Sunset 19.37
Moonrise 04.44
Moonset 12.05

Thursday 4

Sunrise 06.28
Sunset 19.39
Moonrise 05.12
Moonset 13.35

Friday 5

Sunrise 06.25
Sunset 19.41
Moonrise 05.32
Moonset 15.07

Saturday 6

Sunrise 06.23
Sunset 19.42
Moonrise 05.48
Moonset 16.39

Sunday 7

Sunrise 06.21
Sunset 19.44
Moonrise 06.02
Moonset 18.10

Wood Anemone
Folk names: Fairies' Windflower, Lady's Shimmy, Moll O' the Woods, Moon Flower, Smell Foxes, Cuckoo Flower, Drops of Snow & Easter Flower.

Sweet Violet
"It is said that a person can only smell sweet violets once,
as they steal your sense of smell."
It is now known that sweet violets contain beta-ionone, a chemical which temporarily shuts off smell receptors.

Monday 8

Sunrise 06.19
Sunset 19.46
Moonrise 06.15
Moonset 19.42

New Moon 19.20

Tuesday 9

Sunrise 06.17
Sunset 19.47
Moonrise 06.29
Moonset 21.14

Wednesday 10

Sunrise 06.14
Sunset 19.49
Moonrise 06.45
Moonset 22.46

Thursday 11

Sunrise 06.12
Sunset 19.51
Moonrise 07.06
Moonset -- --

Friday 12

Sunrise 06.10
Sunset 19.52
Moonset 00.16
Moonrise 07.36

Saturday 13

Sunrise 06.08
Sunset 19.54
Moonset 01.36
Moonrise 08.17

Sunday 14

Sunrise 06.06
Sunset 19.56
Moonset 02.40
Moonrise 09.13

The Davenport Arms, Woodford, Cheshire.

The Davenport Arms is a quiet country pub not far from Macclesfield. However, it has a less-than-charming history, hence its nickname, 'The Thief's Neck'. The name refers to the Davenport family's coat of arms, which depicts a man with a rope around his neck. The Davenports were foresters to the King and, as such, meted out punishment to the poachers they caught.

It is thought that 'regular courts' were held at the 18th century pub and offending poachers were hanged from a nearby tree. On one such occasion the hangman was sent for whilst the 'guilty' poacher was made ready with a hood being placed over his head. Once the dreadful deed was complete, the hangman removed the hood only to discover that he had hanged his own son!

The pub is also reputed to be home to the ghost of a maid. One unlucky resident was preparing for bed and got undressed, placing his clothes in the wardrobe. Suddenly he felt very uneasy and could not explain why, but he knew it had something to do with the wardrobe. However, when he got out of bed to investigate he found nothing untoward. The next morning the landlord asked if he had slept well and was not surprised to hear that the man had not. He explained that a maid had been murdered in his room 100 years ago and her body had been hidden in the wardrobe!

Monday 15

Sunrise 06.03
Sunset 19.57
Moonset 03.27
Moonrise 10.21

First Quarter 20.13

Tuesday 16

Sunrise 06.01
Sunset 19.59
Moonset 03.59
Moonrise 11.35

Wednesday 17

Sunrise 05.59
Sunset 20.01
Moonset 04.21
Moonrise 12.50

Thursday 18

Sunrise 05.57
Sunset 20.02
Moonset 04.38
Moonrise 14.04

Friday 19

Sunrise 05.55
Sunset 20.04
Moonset 04.50
Moonrise 15.15

Saturday 20

Sunrise 05.53
Sunset 20.06
Moonset 05.00
Moonrise 16.25

Sunday 21

Sunrise 05.51
Sunset 20.07
Moonset 05.10
Moonrise 17.35

Dent-de-lion or Dandelion

This useful plant's name originates from the French, Dent-de-Lion, due to its coarsely-toothed leaves resembling the teeth of a lion. Once a much-encouraged wild plant to have in the garden, it is now often removed as a weed. However, this is a plant that has very many uses as food, wine, root beer, medicine and as a dye. Its roots can be used as a coffee substitute, which has recently become quite popular once more. Its medicinal properties include acting as a diuretic if drunk as tea using the leaves, flowers or roots.The Dandelion represents the Sun, Moon and stars through its transition from flowering to seed. It turns to the sun when its vivid yellow flowers open. Having a long flowering season, these tenacious plants have parachute-like seeds that drift in the wind, often for many miles. Whilst insects, birds and butterflies benefit from its nectar, the dandelion does not need any assistance to become pollinated and form its seeds.

Children have long blown the 'fluffy' seed globes of Dandelions as an indicator of what the time is but another folklore use is to choose a wish or a thought you want to send to someone whilst holding the seed head and then blow to disperse it and so make your wish or thought come true. Dandelions are great indicators of two certain times of the day - 5 am when they open and 8 pm when they close, giving them the name, 'The Shepherd's Clock.' But if the weather is inclement the Dandelion will stay shut until the rain has passed, making it a useful barometer.

Monday 22

Sunrise 05.49
Sunset 20.09
Moonset 05.19
Moonrise 18.45

Earth Day

Tuesday 23

Sunrise 05.47
Sunset 20.11
Moonset 05.30
Moonrise 19.58

St. George's Day (Patron Saint of England)

Wednesday 24

Sunrise 05.45
Sunset 20.12
Moonset 05.42
Moonrise 21.14

'Egg' Moon 00.48

Thursday 25

Sunrise 05.43
Sunset 20.14
Moonset 05.57
Moonrise 22.32

Friday 26

Sunrise 05.41
Sunset 20.16
Moonset 06.18
Moonrise 23.50

Saturday 27

Sunrise 05.39
Sunset 20.17
Moonset 06.48
Moonrise -- --

Sunday 28

Sunrise 05.37
Sunset 20.19
Moonrise 01.02
Moonset 07.33

Cannock Chase

Cannock Chase, known locally as The Chase, is an area of outstanding natural beauty in Staffordshire in the West Midlands. Well-known and loved for its scenery, wildlife and rich history, it offers a tranquil and peaceful environment. However, it is also steeped in folklore tales that include apparitions of a 'black-eyed child', panthers, UFOs, Bigfoot, soldiers, the First Marquess of Anglesey with his hounds, a parachutist who never lands, a gamekeeper, a monk, a cyclist and cryptids.

Castle Ring Hillfort, which is over 2,000 years old, is a popular area known for strange and supernatural phenomena and some believe it is a supernatural portal. Also fuelling the potential for strange sightings, such as the cryptid Pigman, is the fact there was a military base on The Chase during World War Two, about which rumours spread of secret experiments involving human-animal hybrids. Even today, mountain bikers and walkers in the area have been left disturbed by sightings of pale creatures around Castle Ring car park and of a little girl without eyes who appears on pathways and in the wooded areas.

The story of the 'Black-Eyed Child' seems to have begun in the 1970s when a couple out on a walk encountered a little girl asking for help. On seeing her face, with dark holes where her eyes should have been they were overcome by a sense of fear and unease and this feeling is something many have reported even before they see her face. The child is seen in old-fashioned clothing and seemingly transports herself from tree to tree. People who have encountered her have described that they feel hypnotised and are left with headaches and nausea after the encounter.

Many investigators of the paranormal have visited the area to try to discover why there have been so many reports to the police, and now on the internet, of strange sightings. More recently, between 1965 and 1967 three separate incidents of child abduction and murder resulted in reports of the bodies of three young girls being discovered on The Chase. Known as the 'Babes in the Ditch' murders, perhaps these terrible crimes have left an imprint on locals and the land that has made them susceptible to the sightings and stories that come from this beauty spot.

Monday 29

Sunrise 05.35
Sunset 20.21
Moonrise 02.01
Moonset 08.34

Tuesday 30

Sunrise 05.33
Sunset 20.22
Moonrise 02.44
Moonset 09.50

Wednesday 1

Sunrise 05.31
Sunset 20.24
Moonrise 03.15
Moonset 11.16

Third Quarter 12.27 / Beltane / May Day

Thursday 2

Sunrise 05.29
Sunset 20.26
Moonrise 03.37
Moonset 12.45

Friday 3

Sunrise 05.27
Sunset 20.27
Moonrise 03.54
Moonset 14.13

Saturday 4

Sunrise 05.26
Sunset 20.29
Moonrise 04.08
Moonset 15.41

Sunday 5

Sunrise 05.24
Sunset 20.31
Moonrise 04.20
Moonset 17.09

Merry May Day

"Come listen awhile unto what we shall say, concerning the season, the month of May; For the flowers they are springing, and the birds they do sing, And the baziers* are sweet in the morning of May".

Extract from 'New May Song', Swinton May Songs, recorded in Chambers Book of Days 1864
*The bazier is the name given in this part of Lancashire to the auricula, which is usually found in full bloom in April.

Maypoles, having been banned by Cromwell, were joyfully restored in 1660 when Charles II was returned to the throne, and once again became a centre of May Day celebrations. Equally, the crowning of May Queens, accompanied by a May King (often a Jack-in-the-Green), set the scene across many villages as May 1st was marked with merriment and mirth.

On May Day Eve country folk would ramble collecting armfuls of sweet-smelling hawthorn (Mayflower) that had just come into bloom, ready to adorn the tops of maypoles, to make bowers to put above doors and barns and to make into hoops and garlands on May Day morn. A festival that seems steeped in pagan fertility rights, May Day became a day of merrymaking for all ages, as children and adults alike danced around maypoles, lit bonfires (Beltane fires) and truly welcomed the beginning of summer. To us, May Day is a springtime festival but at one time we had only two seasons, summer and winter, which was known as Samhain in Gaelic/Celtic tradition.

In parts of Cornwall in 1826 it is recorded that on May Day Eve at midnight, people went from door to door for a 'junket' with cream and sugar and a piece of rich fruited cake. Cow horns were blown throughout the night and whistles made from May twigs shrilled, as many stayed up to welcome the dawn and bathed in the May morning dew that was known for its magical properties as a beauty treatment.

Monday 6

Sunrise 05.22
Sunset 20.32
Moonrise 04.33
Moonset 18.39

Tuesday 7

Sunrise 05.20
Sunset 20.34
Moonrise 04.48
Moonset 20.11

Wednesday 8

Sunrise 05.19
Sunset 20.35
Moonrise 05.07
Moonset 21.42

New Moon 04.21

Thursday 9

Sunrise 05.17
Sunset 20.37
Moonrise 05.32
Moonset 23.09

Friday 10

Sunrise 05.15
Sunset 20.38
Moonrise 06.08
Moonset -- --

Saturday 11

Sunrise 05.14
Sunset 20.40
Moonset 00.23
Moonrise 06.58

Sunday 12

Sunrise 05.12
Sunset 20.42
Moonset 01.19
Moonrise 08.03

"If a swallow builds a nest on your house, it is a sign of good luck."

"Whatever you are doing, when you first hear the Cuckoo, you will do most frequently all the year." From Norfolk

"Branches of hawthorn fastened to doors and windows keep out witches."

Monday 13

Sunrise 05.11
Sunset 20.43
Moonset 01.58
Moonrise 09.17

Tuesday 14

Sunrise 05.09
Sunset 20.45
Moonset 02.25
Moonrise 10.33

Wednesday 15

Sunrise 05.08
Sunset 20.46
Moonset 02.43
Moonrise 11.49

First Quarter 12.48

Thursday 16

Sunrise 05.06
Sunset 20.48
Moonset 02.57
Moonrise 13.01

Friday 17

Sunrise 05.05
Sunset 20.49
Moonset 03.08
Moonrise 14.12

Saturday 18

Sunrise 05.03
Sunset 20.50
Moonset 03.18
Moonrise 15.21

Sunday 19

Sunrise 05.02
Sunset 20.52
Moonset 03.28
Moonrise 16.31

Whit Sunday

Dead Woman's Grave

On the quiet parish boundary of Codsall in Staffordshire, close to the border with Shropshire, lies the grave of an unknown woman, which has been recorded since the sixteenth century. Some believe the poor woman's fate was meted out by a lynch mob. According to the legend that has grown around the crossroads, she was a vagrant and had stolen some apples, so the locals took the law into their own hands and hanged her from a nearby tree, then buried her where she fell.
However, a more likely scenario is that this is the burial site of a suicide victim. People who took their own lives, no matter how tragic their story, were not allowed to be buried in a churchyard and were often buried at crossroads, sometimes with a stake driven through their hearts as a warning to others.

By 1882, victims of suicide were allowed to be buried in churchyards, although by law this had to be done between 9 pm and midnight. It was not until 1961 that suicide ceased to be a crime. However, as recently as 2015, Church of England clergy were not allowed to conduct funeral services for those 'of sound mind' who committed suicide.
Whatever the fate of this poor lady, her life will always be commemorated by the roadside plaque that marks her resting place.

Monday 20

Sunrise 05.01
Sunset 20.53
Moonset 03.38
Moonrise 17.43

Tuesday 21

Sunrise 04.59
Sunset 20.55
Moonset 03.49
Moonrise 18.58

Wednesday 22

Sunrise 04.58
Sunset 20.56
Moonset 04.03
Moonrise 20.16

Thursday 23

Sunrise 04.57
Sunset 20.57
Moonset 04.22
Moonrise 21.35

'Milk' Moon 14.53

Friday 24

Sunrise 04.56
Sunset 20.59
Moonset 04.50
Moonrise 22.51

Saturday 25

Sunrise 04.55
Sunset 21.00
Moonset 05.30
Moonrise 23.55

Sunday 26

Sunrise 04.54
Sunset 21.01
Moonset 06.26
Moonrise -- --

Bluebells

Such is our love of the native British bluebell that people have long since travelled to see them and to breathe in the scent of this harbinger of summer. Before our woodlands come into full leaf, the bluebell makes the most of dappled sunlight and is often thought of as a signifier of a surviving tract of ancient woodland. Bluebell Trains once ran through the woodlands in the Chiltern Hills and, in East Sussex, a particular stretch is known as The Bluebell Railway.

This flower was once associated with St. George, probably due to its flowering at the time of St. George's Day on April 23rd. It is believed to have 'arrived' in Britain after the last Ice Age.

In the Bronze Age, Bluebell roots were used to make a glue to fix feathers as arrow flights; and in Tudor times, to make starch to stiffen collars and ruffs. Bluebell root glue has also been used throughout the centuries by bookbinders.

Folk remedy uses for; tuberculosis, spider bites and leprosy.

Sayings: *"On picking a bluebell say "Bluebell, bluebell, bring me some luck before tomorrow night;" then slip it into your shoe and you will get good luck."*

"If you wear a wreath of bluebells you can compel a person to tell the truth."

"If you turn a bluebell flower inside out, you will win the heart of your true love."

"Bluebells planted by your door will ring to tell of unwanted visitors."

Folk names listed in "The Englishman's Flora" by Geoffrey Grigson (1955) *Blue Bonnets, Blue Bottle, Blue Goggles, Blue Granfer Greygles, Blue Rocket, Blue Trumpet, Bummack, Bummuck, Crawtraes, Crakefeet, Crawfeet, Cross flower, Crow-bells, Crow-Flower, Crowfoot, Crow picker, Crows Legs, Crowtoes, Cuckoo, Cuckoo Flower, Cuckoo's Boots, Cuckoo's Stockings, Culvers, Culverkeys, Fairy Bells, Goosey Gander, Gowk's Hose, Granfer Gregors, Grammar Greygles, Granfer Griddlesticks, Greygles, Harebell, Pride of the Wood, Ring O'Bells, Rooks Flower, Single Gussies, Snake's flower, Snapgrass, Wild Hyacinth and Wood Bells.*

May / June Spring

Monday 27
Sunrise 04.53
Sunset 21.03
Moonrise 00.44
Moonset 07.40

Spring Bank Holiday

Tuesday 28
Sunrise 04.52
Sunset 21.04
Moonrise 01.18
Moonset 09.04

Wednesday 29
Sunrise 04.51
Sunset 21.05
Moonrise 01.43
Moonset 10.31

Oak Apple Day

Thursday 30
Sunrise 04.50
Sunset 21.06
Moonrise 02.00
Moonset 11.58

Third Quarter 18.12

Friday 31
Sunrise 04.49
Sunset 21.07
Moonrise 02.15
Moonset 13.24

Saturday 1
Sunrise 04.48
Sunset 21.08
Moonrise 02.27
Moonset 14.50

Sunday 2
Sunrise 04.47
Sunset 21.09
Moonrise 02.40
Moonset 16.16

Old English Riddles

Hrægl mīn swīgað, þonne ic hrūsan trede,
oþþe þā wīc būge, oþþe wado drēfe.
Hwīlum mec āhebbað ofer hæleþa byht
hyrste mīne, ond þēos hēa lyft,
ond mec þonne wīde wolcna strengu
ofer folc byreð. Frætwe mīne swōgað hlūde ond swinsiað,
torhte singað, þonne ic getenge ne bēom
flōde ond foldan, fērende gæst.

My garment is silent when I tread upon the earth
or reside in my dwelling or stir up the waters.
Sometimes my apparel and this high air
lift me over the dwellings of men, and the strength of the clouds carries me far
over the people. My ornaments resound loudly and make music,
sing clearly, when I am not resting on
water and ground, a travelling spirit.

Riddles were an important element in Anglo Saxon literature. Many were written in the 7th century by Aldhelm, who was an early Christian scholar and Bishop from Wessex. The Old English riddle above is known as Riddle number 7 and it is thought that the answer is a Swan. It is from the 10th century Exeter Book which is one of the most important collections of Anglo Saxon literature. In 2016 it was cited by UNESCO as "one of the world's principal cultural artefacts".

Monday 3
Sunrise 04.47
Sunset 21.10
Moonrise 02.53
Moonset 17.44

Tuesday 4
Sunrise 04.46
Sunset 21.11
Moonrise 03.10
Moonset 19.14

Wednesday 5
Sunrise 04.46
Sunset 21.12
Moonrise 03.31
Moonset 20.42

Thursday 6
Sunrise 04.45
Sunset 21.13
Moonrise 04.02
Moonset 22.02

New Moon 13.37

Friday 7
Sunrise 04.44
Sunset 21.14
Moonrise 04.45
Moonset 23.06

Saturday 8
Sunrise 04.44
Sunset 21.15
Moonrise 05.44
Moonset 23.53

Sunday 9
Sunrise 04.44
Sunset 21.16
Moonrise 06.56
Moonset -- --

St. John's Wort is also known as Solstice Wort, since it blooms at the time of the Summer Solstice, and June 24th (Midsummer's Day which is also St. John's Day) is the best time to harvest this long-revered healing plant. It is best known for alleviating depression but has magickal properties as protection against elves, devils, demons and all evils.

Now is the time to make a sun wheel in readiness for the coming Summer Solstice. You can use twigs tied at the centre to form the spokes of a wheel and weave yellow, orange and red threads to symbolise our sun. One of the traditions was to make large pitch-doused 'wheels' that would be set alight and rolled down hills to represent the declining sun.

Midsummer is known as Golowan in the Cornish language and is a time for celebrations that centre on the lighting of large community bonfires. People would link in circles, hand-in-hand around the fires to preserve themselves against witchcraft and as the fire burnt low, some of them would leap over the embers to ensure their protection.

Monday 10
Sunrise 04.43
Sunset 21.16
Moonset 00.25
Moonrise 08.13

Tuesday 11
Sunrise 04.43
Sunset 21.17
Moonset 00.47
Moonrise 09.30

Wednesday 12
Sunrise 04.43
Sunset 21.18
Moonset 01.03
Moonrise 10.45

Thursday 13
Sunrise 04.43
Sunset 21.18
Moonset 01.15
Moonrise 11.56

Friday 14
Sunrise 04.42
Sunset 21.19
Moonset 01.25
Moonrise 13.06

First Quarter 06.18

Saturday 15
Sunrise 04.42
Sunset 21.19
Moonset 01.35
Moonrise 14.16

Sunday 16
Sunrise 04.42
Sunset 21.20
Moonset 01.44
Moonrise 15.26

Father's Day

The Monkey Man

The Monkey Man was the name given to the hideous creature that is said to appear at Bridge 39 on the Shropshire Union Canal, near Woodseaves in Staffordshire.

The apparition is thought to be that of a boatman who drowned in the 19th century, although the way it was described in 1879 - a strange black creature with enormous eyes - was far more sinister. The account was given by a local man who had been tasked with delivering a cart of luggage from nearby Ranton to Newport, across the border in Shropshire.

On his return journey, as he crossed the canal near Norbury at around 10 pm, the beast sprang out of some bushes and landed on the back of his horse. When he tried to whip the creature, he found his whip passed through its body. He then fell off his horse in fear and it galloped off with the creature still clinging to its back. Apparently the man was so terrified he took to his bed for two days!

Another sighting, in the 1980s, was recounted by a holidaymaker who was at the tiller as he passed below Bridge 39. As he looked up, he saw what he could only describe as "a huge black, hairy monkey" looking down upon him. However, by the time he had called his family, he had passed under the bridge and the creature was nowhere to be seen!

Monday 17

Sunrise 04.42
Sunset 21.20
Moonset 01.55
Moonrise 16.39

Tuesday 18

Sunrise 04.42
Sunset 21.20
Moonset 02.08
Moonrise 17.56

Wednesday 19

Sunrise 04.42
Sunset 21.21
Moonset 02.25
Moonrise 19.15

Thursday 20

Sunrise 04.43
Sunset 21.21
Moonset 02.49
Moonrise 20.33

Litha / Summer Solstice 21.50 / Summer officially begins

Friday 21

Sunrise 04.43
Sunset 21.21
Moonset 03.24
Moonrise 21.44

Saturday 22

Sunrise 04.43
Sunset 21.21
Moonset 04.15
Moonrise 22.39

'Flower' Moon 02.07 / Midsummer's Day

Sunday 23

Sunrise 04.43
Sunset 21.21
Moonset 05.24
Moonrise 23.19

Summer Solstice

It is the longest day of the year and, for many, marks the arrival of summer, although some consider Beltane (May Day) to be the beginning of summer. As with all thing's folklore, many local traditions and beliefs contradict the significance of this day and the way it is celebrated - as nothing is set in stone. However, stone circles are set stones, and, for many, it is important to be at ancient sites such as these to see the sunrise on this day. There is no hard evidence of the connection between these ancient sites and the Summer Solstice, other than a few of them, in part, aligning with the current trajectory of our sun, but many like to believe its origins go back to Neolithic times. Certainly, for our farming ancestors the Summer Solstice could signify the transition and growth of the crop cycles and the day may well have been marked by bonfires to ensure a healthy harvest and remind the sun to shine.

Strangely, Midsummer's Day is marked only three days later. This is the time when people believed spirits, fey folk and magick were abroad. Bonfires, sometimes called 'Aestival' fires, were lit, known as "setting the watch", and these would keep evil at bay and bring fertility to the land. Their smoke would also purify and bless the cattle returning to summer pastures and give power to our sun. It became traditional for the foolhardy to jump the midsummer bonfire, which was said to bring good luck.

Folklore Beliefs - the days leading up to midsummer are the last days to hear the cuckoo call and to hear a cuckoo on Midsummer's Day was considered very unlucky.

To pick a fern at midsummer and keep its seeds in your pocket was to render yourself invisible.

If you see a white butterfly at midsummer, you will eat white bread for the rest of your life. This was written at a time when white bread was a luxury and brown bread was the norm and considered lowly.

Tradition – People would decorate their houses with birch twigs, St John's Wort and roses to mark the time of year.

Monday 24

Sunrise 04.44
Sunset 21.21
Moonset 06.47
Moonrise 23.47

Tuesday 25

Sunrise 04.44
Sunset 21.21
Moonset 08.16
Moonrise -- --

Wednesday 26

Sunrise 04.45
Sunset 21.21
Moonrise 00.07
Moonset 09.45

Thursday 27

Sunrise 04.45
Sunset 21.21
Moonrise 00.22
Moonset 11.12

Friday 28

Sunrise 04.46
Sunset 21.21
Moonrise 00.35
Moonset 12.37

Third Quarter 22.53

Saturday 29

Sunrise 04.46
Sunset 21.21
Moonrise 00.47
Moonset 14.02

Sunday 30

Sunrise 04.47
Sunset 21.21
Moonrise 01.00
Moonset 15.28

The 'Wishing Stone' at St Nicholas's Priory Tresco

On the island of Tresco are the Abbey gardens, which house a great many things of interest. Within these wonderful subtropical gardens, which are a haven for red squirrels and home to the elusive Golden Pheasant, is a collection of ships' figureheads and an 11th century abbey. It is near the site of the abbey that a curious holed stone can be found. This upright stone, approximately four feet in height, has two holes, one above the other. Folklore suggests this is an old Druidical betrothal stone which was in use well before the abbey was built. Young couples who wanted to be betrothed would each push a hand through one of the holes then join them together to "plight their troth".

This type of stone may also have been used for the purpose of making a wish or breaking a spell. To do this, a ring or other valued item would be passed through the holes as incantations were said.

"The holed stone near the church is one of four examples from Scilly of this very rare class of prehistoric ritual monument, whose distribution is concentrated in the western tip of Cornwall and Scilly. Although not in its original position, its present setting, near the early Christian memorial slab and the upright gravestones in the church's post-medieval cemetery, gives a good illustration of the long period over which upright stone slabs have held a strong religious and funerary significance."

Extract from the scheduled monument record.

July Summer

Monday 1
Sunrise 04.47
Sunset 21.20
Moonrise 01.15
Moonset 16.55

Tuesday 2
Sunrise 04.48
Sunset 21.20
Moonrise 01.34
Moonset 18.22

Wednesday 3
Sunrise 04.49
Sunset 21.19
Moonrise 02.00
Moonset 19.44

Thursday 4
Sunrise 04.50
Sunset 21.19
Moonrise 02.38
Moonset 20.54

Friday 5
Sunrise 04.51
Sunset 21.18
Moonrise 03.30
Moonset 21.47

New Moon 23.57

Saturday 6
Sunrise 04.51
Sunset 21.18
Moonrise 04.37
Moonset 22.24

Sunday 7
Sunrise 04.52
Sunset 21.17
Moonrise 05.53
Moonset 22.49

The tale of the 'Shapwick monster' originates from 1706, when a fishmonger travelling to Bere Regis in Dorset accidentally dropped a crab. Villagers had never seen such a creature before and thought it was a devil. They rounded on the crab with pitchforks to drive it out of the village. The fishmonger, on realising he had dropped the crab, retraced his steps. only to find the strange sight of the villagers surrounding the crab. He picked up the crab to the amazement of the crowd and spread the story of the 'simple' folk of Shapwick. There is said to be a Crab Farm in Shapwick commemorating this event.

Monday 8

Sunrise 04.53
Sunset 21.16
Moonrise 07.11
Moonset 23.07

Tuesday 9

Sunrise 04.54
Sunset 21.16
Moonrise 08.27
Moonset 23.21

Wednesday 10

Sunrise 04.55
Sunset 21.15
Moonrise 09.40
Moonset 23.32

Thursday 11

Sunrise 04.56
Sunset 21.14
Moonrise 10.51
Moonset 23.42

Friday 12

Sunrise 04.58
Sunset 21.13
Moonrise 12.01
Moonset 23.51

Bank Holiday in Northern Ireland

Saturday 13

Sunrise 04.59
Sunset 21.12
Moonrise 13.10
Moonset -- --

First Quarter 23.48

Sunday 14

Sunrise 05.00
Sunset 21.11
Moonset 00.01
Moonrise 14.22

Rudston Monolith

The tiny village of Rudston in the East Riding of Yorkshire is home to the tallest monolith in the British Isles, measuring over 25 feet. The top appears to be broken, but if it was originally pointed it would have been 28 feet tall. It stands in the churchyard of All Saints Church and shows how important this site was to our ancestors well before Christianity.

There is a myth that when the church was built on this pagan site, the devil was so angered that he threw a giant stone spear at the church but, by divine intervention, it veered off course. Maybe this is how the top of the monolith was broken off?

During excavations in the 18th century many skulls were found around the base of the stone, leading some to believe that human sacrifice may once have taken place at the site.

During this time a lead cap was added to protect the stone from further deterioration. Further analysis of the stone has shown that only half of it may be above ground, with a further 25 feet beneath the soil.

The stone was brought to the site 4,000 years ago from a quarry in Cleveland about 40 miles away, and it is thought it was erected here as a focal point for the surrounding area, which is filled with ancient sites.

Monday 15

Sunrise 05.01
Sunset 21.10
Moonset 00.13
Moonrise 15.36

St. Swithun's Day

Tuesday 16

Sunrise 05.02
Sunset 21.09
Moonset 00.28
Moonrise 16.53

Wednesday 17

Sunrise 05.03
Sunset 21.08
Moonset 00.48
Moonrise 18.12

Thursday 18

Sunrise 05.05
Sunset 21.07
Moonset 01.17
Moonrise 19.26

Friday 19

Sunrise 05.06
Sunset 21.06
Moonset 02.01
Moonrise 20.29

Saturday 20

Sunrise 05.07
Sunset 21.05
Moonset 03.03
Moonrise 21.15

Sunday 21

Sunrise 05.09
Sunset 21.03
Moonset 04.22
Moonrise 21.48

'Hay' Moon 11.17

The Fox

Nature Notes
Foxes are the only type of 'dog' to have retractable claws similar to a cat's. They are found in different forms all around the world. The Red Fox is an omnivore and will mainly eat small rodents when available, but during the autumn fruit can amount to 100 per cent of its diet.

Superstition
In Oxfordshire it was once thought that to cure children of whooping cough you should take them to visit the home of someone who had a fox, carrying some milk with you. The fox was then allowed to drink as much of the milk as it liked and what remained was given to the children to drink, thus curing them of their cough.

Myth
Foxes are thought to be very wise, and this example shows why the idea has persisted. A fox who had become afflicted with fleas found a tuft of sheep's wool in the field, then went into a river, holding the wool in his teeth. As the fox went deeper into the water, the fleas made their way up his body until they had nowhere else to go but the tuft of wool. The wily fox then let go of the wool so it was carried away by the current of the river, thus ridding himself of the fleas.

Monday 22

Sunrise 05.10
Sunset 21.02
Moonset 05.52
Moonrise 22.11

Tuesday 23

Sunrise 05.11
Sunset 21.01
Moonset 07.24
Moonrise 22.28

Wednesday 24

Sunrise 05.13
Sunset 20.59
Moonset 08.55
Moonrise 22.42

Thursday 25

Sunrise 05.14
Sunset 20.58
Moonset 10.23
Moonrise 22.54

Friday 26

Sunrise 05.16
Sunset 20.57
Moonset 11.49
Moonrise 23.07

Saturday 27

Sunrise 05.17
Sunset 20.55
Moonset 13.16
Moonrise 23.21

Sunday 28

Sunrise 05.18
Sunset 20.54
Moonset 14.43
Moonrise 23.39

Third Quarter 03.51

Rainbows

Nowadays rainbow folklore is often positive; people may like to make a wish when they see a rainbow, or hope to find a pot of gold at the rainbow's end. Among animal lovers, The Rainbow Bridge is believed by many to be the pathway their beloved pets will take when they die, to reach a nirvana or heaven.

However, there is a darker side to rainbow folklore.

In Orkney, there is a superstition that "A rainbow with both ends on one island is a sign of death" (1909); and in County Wexford, "If both ends of a rainbow fall in the same 'townland', death will follow"(1899). In Shetland, a rainbow arched over a house meant there would soon be a death in it. (Saxeby, Shetland Lore 1932)

Children and children's rhymes are particularly associated with rainbows.

"Rainbowie, rainbowie
Dinna rain o'me
Rain o' John o' Groat's house
Or far beyond the sea."
(Caithness 1895)

It was also believed, mainly by children, that a rainbow could be 'crossed out' or made to disappear. Whether this was due to a worry it would bring bad luck, or the misconception that rainbows caused rain, is unclear.

"Rainbow rainbow bring me luck
If you don't, I'll break you up."
(Essex)

Monday 29

Sunrise 05.20
Sunset 20.52
Moonset 16.10
Moonrise -- --

Tuesday 30

Sunrise 05.21
Sunset 20.51
Moonrise 00.02
Moonset 17.33

Wednesday 31

Sunrise 05.23
Sunset 20.49
Moonrise 00.35
Moonset 18.46

Thursday 1

Sunrise 05.24
Sunset 20.47
Moonrise 01.22
Moonset 19.43

Lammas

Friday 2

Sunrise 05.26
Sunset 20.46
Moonrise 02.23
Moonset 20.24

Saturday 3

Sunrise 05.27
Sunset 20.44
Moonrise 03.36
Moonset 20.53

Sunday 4

Sunrise 05.29
Sunset 20.42
Moonrise 04.54
Moonset 21.13

New Moon 12.13

The First Harvest

Lughnasadh, or Lughnasa, is a Gaelic festival which marks the beginning of the harvest season, the decline of summer and the approach of winter. It commemorates Lugh, the god of light and wisdom, and is one of the four great fire festivals in the Celtic year.
Marked in Ireland as a holiday on August 1st, Lughnasadh would once have involved a month of festivities centred on a bountiful harvest, between mid-July and mid-August. Bilberry Sunday, Garland Sunday and Crom Dubh Sunday probably all stem from such festivities. These days mark the gathering of ripened bilberries, placing flower garlands at holy wells and harvesting grain, which brought an end to the 'hungry season'. This period of celebration evolved and became known as Lammas across much of the British Isles, as Christian culture supplanted pagan beliefs and the old gods were forgotten as the tradition of Lammas fairs became more widespread. The Lammas fair in Kirkwall, Orkney, lasted 11 days, during which young couples, known as Lammas brothers and sisters, would forge a relationship to 'try each other out', with a view to either a long-term commitment or a parting of the ways.
Lammas was a time when reverse faerie 'snatching' could take place. Mortals would place children they suspected of being changelings in a hole overnight, then return in the morning to find the mortal baby returned to its parents and the fae child back in the faerie realm.

Nature Notes; The first harvest of grain is collected and Lammas loaves are made, using intricate designs. Nowadays, modern grain crops are often planted and harvested earlier, which is having a detrimental effect on birds, plants, insects and wildlife.
Superstition; *"A loaf once cut should never be turned or bad luck will ensue."*
Saying; *"Harvest will come and then every farmer is rich."*

Monday 5

Sunrise 05.30
Sunset 20.40
Moonrise 06.11
Moonset 21.28

Summer Bank Holiday in Scotland

Tuesday 6

Sunrise 05.32
Sunset 20.39
Moonrise 07.25
Moonset 21.39

Wednesday 7

Sunrise 05.34
Sunset 20.37
Moonrise 08.37
Moonset 21.49

Thursday 8

Sunrise 05.35
Sunset 20.35
Moonrise 09.47
Moonset 21.59

Friday 9

Sunrise 05.37
Sunset 20.33
Moonrise 10.56
Moonset 22.08

Saturday 10

Sunrise 05.38
Sunset 20.31
Moonrise 12.07
Moonset 22.19

Sunday 11

Sunrise 05.40
Sunset 20.29
Moonrise 13.19
Moonset 22.32

A visit to the seaside in August was a tradition for many in the British Isles as factories used to shut down for a fortnight. Day trips to the seaside were very popular in times when annual leave was limited. It was believed that taking in the sea air was beneficial to health. In Wales it was believed that if you took a sip of sea water each morning from childhood then you would live to a 'ripe old age'. The Welsh also believed that a bunch of seaweed kept hanging on the kitchen door would keep away all evil spirits. Whereas in Devon people would collect and dry seaweed which they would put in a vase on the mantlepiece to prevent the house catching fire.

Monday 12

Sunrise 05.41
Sunset 20.27
Moonrise 14.34
Moonset 22.49

First Quarter 16.18

Tuesday 13

Sunrise 05.43
Sunset 20.25
Moonrise 15.51
Moonset 23.13

Wednesday 14

Sunrise 05.45
Sunset 20.24
Moonrise 17.07
Moonset 23.49

Thursday 15

Sunrise 05.46
Sunset 20.22
Moonrise 18.14
Moonset -- --

Friday 16

Sunrise 05.48
Sunset 20.20
Moonset 00.41
Moonrise 19.07

Saturday 17

Sunrise 05.49
Sunset 20.18
Moonset 01.53
Moonrise 19.46

Sunday 18

Sunrise 05.51
Sunset 20.15
Moonset 03.19
Moonrise 20.13

Upper Sheringham Mermaid

Most stories of mermaids tell of how they lure sailors or unsuspecting folk to their deaths through their siren's call, but in Upper Sheringham, in Norfolk, it was the mermaid who was lured to a church by the sound of parishioners singing. It is said that the mermaid dragged herself overland, for over a mile, because she heard the 'sweet singing'. According to the legend found in the church, she struggled to push open the heavy door only to be told, according to the legend found in the church, by the Bedale (the church's usher) that she wasn't welcome. He said: *"Git e warn owt, we carn't hey noo mearmeads in 'are!"* and slammed the door in her face, as it was believed that mermaids had no soul. But the mermaid was undeterred by the Bedale and slipped into the back of the church through the north

door, into the back pew, joining the congregation.

If you visit All Saints Church today you can still find her, as a carving, on one of the 15th century pews in this 900-year-old church.

Superstition:

North doors in churches were often referred to as the 'Devil's door'. It is said the north door would be left open during a baptism so that, once the devil had left the baby as the holy water was poured on its head, he could leave the church.

Monday 19

Sunrise 05.53
Sunset 20.13
Moonset 04.52
Moonrise 20.32

'Grain' Moon 19.25

Tuesday 20

Sunrise 05.54
Sunset 20.11
Moonset 06.25
Moonrise 20.47

Wednesday 21

Sunrise 05.56
Sunset 20.09
Moonset 07.57
Moonrise 21.00

Thursday 22

Sunrise 05.57
Sunset 20.07
Moonset 09.27
Moonrise 21.13

Friday 23

Sunrise 05.59
Sunset 20.05
Moonset 10.57
Moonrise 21.27

Saturday 24

Sunrise 06.00
Sunset 20.03
Moonset 12.26
Moonrise 21.43

Sunday 25

Sunrise 06.02
Sunset 20.01
Moonset 13.56
Moonrise 22.05

Harvest Moon

"When you go to bed place under your pillow a prayerbook open at the part of the matrimonial service which says, 'With this ring I thee wed'; place on it a key, a ring, a flower and a sprig of willow, a small heart cake, a crust of bread and the following cards - ten of clubs, nine of hearts, ace of spades and ace of diamonds. Wrap all of these in a handkerchief of gauze or muslin and, on getting into bed, cross your hands and say:

'Luna, every woman's friend,
To me thy goodness condescend;
Let me this night in visions see
Emblems of my destiny.'

If you then dream of storms, trouble will betide you; if the storms end in a fine calm, so will your fate; if of a ring or of the ace of diamonds, marriage; bread, an industrious life; flowers, joy; willow, treachery in love; spades, death; clubs, a foreign land; diamonds, money; keys, that you will rise to great trust and power; birds, that you will have many children; and geese, that you will marry more than once."

From Observations on the Popular Antiquities of Great Britain by John Brand 1854

Monday 26

Sunrise 06.04
Sunset 19.59
Moonset 15.22
Moonrise 22.35

Third Quarter 10.25 / Late Summer Bank Holiday

Tuesday 27

Sunrise 06.05
Sunset 19.56
Moonset 16.39
Moonrise 23.17

Wednesday 28

Sunrise 06.07
Sunset 19.54
Moonset 17.42
Moonrise -- --

Thursday 29

Sunrise 06.08
Sunset 19.52
Moonrise 00.15
Moonset 18.27

Friday 30

Sunrise 06.10
Sunset 19.50
Moonrise 01.24
Moonset 18.58

Saturday 31

Sunrise 06.12
Sunset 19.48
Moonrise 02.40
Moonset 19.20

Sunday 1

Sunrise 06.13
Sunset 19.45
Moonrise 03.57
Moonset 19.35

St. Peter's Well, Peterchurch, Herefordshire

We found a wonderful, and rare, working ancient well-head in a field just outside the village of Peterchurch. Its date of origin is unknown, but it is similar to a few other examples, dating from early Celtic times, which mark pagan springs.

The spring, which flows freely, still provides water for the village and creates Wellbrook. This very high-quality water, which comes from an exceptionally deep aquifer, is rich in minerals and was once considered a curative for rheumatism and sore eyes.

Folklorist Mary Ella Leather wrote in 'Folklore of Herefordshire' that there were once three springs on the site. *"The two together, above the large well, were good for eye troubles: into these pins were thrown."* In Mary's time these two springs were closed, leaving the spring we can see today.

Under the well-head, in a bathing area that has now gone, people would immerse themselves in the waters to help alleviate or cure their symptoms.

The spring is situated on an ancient borderland between Wales and England, once known as Ergyng. The people who once inhabited the area would have had great reverence for this site and may have placed the beautifully-carved well-head as a mark of its importance.

In a nearby wood above the well stands an iron cross, which some people believe to be a marker that the site was beginning to feel less pagan and more Christian. In 1933 it was reported that baptisms had been performed there 'in recent times'.

September

Monday 2

Sunrise 06.15
Sunset 19.43
Moonrise 05.12
Moonset 19.48

Tuesday 3

Sunrise 06.16
Sunset 19.41
Moonrise 06.25
Moonset 19.58

New Moon 02.55

Wednesday 4

Sunrise 06.18
Sunset 19.39
Moonrise 07.35
Moonset 20.07

Thursday 5

Sunrise 06.20
Sunset 19.36
Moonrise 08.45
Moonset 20.16

Friday 6

Sunrise 06.21
Sunset 19.34
Moonrise 09.54
Moonset 20.26

Saturday 7

Sunrise 06.23
Sunset 19.32
Moonrise 1.06
Moonset 20.38

Sunday 8

Sunrise 06.24
Sunset 19.30
Moonrise 12.19
Moonset 20.53

"On eating an apple, it should first be peeled in one continuous stroke and the peel thrown over the left shoulder. The letter the peel forms indicates the first letter of a future lover's name."

"To pick blackberries after St. Michael's Day (29th) was to 'court calamity'. For on that day the Devil spits on blackberries, and anyone eating after that date will suffer some grave misfortune."

"The sharing of the last portion of grain on the farm is called 'cutting the gander's neck' and betokens plenty." - Shropshire

September   Summer

Monday 9
Sunrise 06.26
Sunset 19.27
Moonrise 13.35
Moonset 21.14

Tuesday 10
Sunrise 06.28
Sunset 19.25
Moonrise 14.50
Moonset 21.44

Wednesday 11
Sunrise 06.29
Sunset 19.23
Moonrise 16.00
Moonset 22.27

First Quarter   07.05

Thursday 12
Sunrise 06.31
Sunset 19.20
Moonrise 16.58
Moonset 23.29

Friday 13
Sunrise 06.32
Sunset 19.18
Moonrise 17.42
Moonset -- --

Saturday 14
Sunrise 06.34
Sunset 19.16
Moonset 00.47
Moonrise 18.13

Sunday 15
Sunrise 06.36
Sunset 19.14
Moonset 02.15
Moonrise 18.35

The Devil's Nutting Day

The Devil's Nutting Day has two dates on which it is commemorated; September 14th (Holy Cross Day) and September 21st (St. Matthew's Day). It was said that if you went collecting hazelnuts on these days you would meet the Devil. (It was also said that if you went 'nutting' on a Sunday, you would also meet the Devil.) This superstition probably began in an attempt to discourage older children from indulging in amorous activities on holy days when they were alone together in the woods!

"The Devil, as some folk say,
A nutting goes on Holy Rood day.
Let women then their children keep
At home that day, better asleep
They were, or cattle for to tend
Then nutting go, and meet thy Fiend;
But if they'll not be ruled by this,
Blame me not if they go amiss."
From Poor Robin's Almanac of 1693

During the 17th century 'going nutting' crops up regularly in songs and plays of the time and became a byword for seduction. According to a popular saying from the 1660s;

" A good year for nuts, a good year for babies."

Near Alcester in Warwickshire there is a hill named The Devil's Nightcap, which was said to be formed when the Devil, whilst out 'nutting', happened upon the Virgin Mary. Apparently, he was so surprised by the meeting that he dropped his bag of nuts, which then formed the hill.

In Warwickshire, anything dirty was said to be *"the colour of the Devil's nutting bag"*. Similarly, in Sussex, it would be described as *"as black as the Devil's nutting bag"*.

September   Summer / Autumn

Monday 16

Sunrise 06.37
Sunset 19.11
Moonset 03.48
Moonrise 18.52

Tuesday 17

Sunrise 06.37
Sunset 19.09
Moonset 05.21
Moonrise 19.06

Wednesday 18

Sunrise 06.40
Sunset 19.07
Moonset 06.53
Moonrise 19.19

'Fruit' Moon 03.34

Thursday 19

Sunrise 06.42
Sunset 19.04
Moonset 08.25
Moonrise 19.32

Friday 20

Sunrise 06.44
Sunset 19.02
Moonset 09.58
Moonrise 19.47

Saturday 21

Sunrise 06.45
Sunset 19.00
Moonset 11.32
Moonrise 20.07

Sunday 22

Sunrise 06.47
Sunset 18.57
Moonset 13.03
Moonrise 20.34

Autumn Equinox 13.43 / Autumn officially begins

Balance is Restored (for a brief moment)

The Autumnal Equinox is the halfway point between the longest and shortest days of the year.

For us in the northern hemisphere, daylight will dwindle until the Winter Solstice, due to our sun taking a lower path in the sky. However, it is not all doom and gloom, as the diminishing sunlight makes our trees start changing into their autumn coats, featuring shades of red, orange, ochre and yellow, before finally dropping their leaves so they are in their bare state for winter.

The months of autumn give us atmospheric early morning mists, magickal fungi, Michaelmas Daisies, architectural seed heads and hips and haws to make syrups, wines, gins, teas and tinctures. Autumn is also the season of chutney and jam making. Fruits, nuts and hops are all ripe for picking and pantries belonging to seasoned foragers, home cooks and healers can become very full as they make use of 'wild food'. The Autumn Equinox, in the 'Wheel of the Year', is often called Mabon (a god of Welsh mythology) or Second Harvest and is a time to welcome bountiful autumn. Perhaps this autumn we could try to become a little more attuned to the season by eating seasonal and local produce. Traditionally, autumn is a season of preparation, when our ancestors preserved foods, collected fuel, put fields into a state of rest and made the most of the daylight hours before the dark days of winter.

Seasonal folklore; *"Sleeping with rosehips under your pillow is thought to protect against bad dreams".*

September   Autumn

Monday 23
Sunrise 06.48
Sunset 18.55
Moonset 14.27
Moonrise 21.13

Tuesday 24
Sunrise 06.50
Sunset 18.53
Moonset 15.37
Moonrise 22.06

Third Quarter 19.49

Wednesday 25
Sunrise 06.52
Sunset 18.50
Moonset 16.28
Moonrise 23.13

Thursday 26
Sunrise 06.53
Sunset 18.48
Moonset 17.03
Moonrise -- --

Friday 27
Sunrise 06.55
Sunset 18.46
Moonrise 00.29
Moonset 17.27

Saturday 28
Sunrise 06.56
Sunset 18.44
Moonrise 01.46
Moonset 17.44

Sunday 29
Sunrise 06.58
Sunset 18.41
Moonrise 03.01
Moonset 17.57

Michaelmas Day (Quarter Day)

The Three Witches Cauldron

In the "Scottish Play" Macbeth (1606) by William Shakespeare there is a famous scene of three witches casting a spell.

"Round about the cauldron go;
In the poison'd entrails throw.
Toad, that under cold stone
Days and nights hast thirty one
Swelter'd venom sleeping got,
Boil thou first i' the charmed pot.
Double, double toil and trouble;
Fire burn and cauldron bubble.
Fillet of a fenny snake,
In the cauldron boil and bake;
Eye of newt, and toe of frog,
Wool of bat, and tongue of dog,
Adder's fork,
and blind-worm's sting,
Lizard's leg, and howlet's wing,
For a charm of powerful trouble,
Like a hell-broth boil and bubble.
Double, double toil and trouble;

Fire burn and cauldron bubble.
Scale of dragon, tooth of wolf,
Witches' mummy, maw and gulf
Of the ravin'd salt-sea shark,
Root of hemlock digg'd i' the dark,
Liver of blaspheming Jew,
Gall of goat, and slips of yew
Sliver'd in the moon's eclipse,
Nose of Turk, and Tartar's lips,
Finger of birth-strangled babe
Ditch-deliver'd by a drab,
Make the gruel thick and slab:
Add thereto a tiger's chaudron,
For the ingredients
of our cauldron.
Double, double toil and trouble;
Fire burn and cauldron bubble."

Whilst many of the strange items being added to the cauldron may be for dramatic effect, many have been identified as ancient terms for herbs, flowers and plants that were known and used by herbal healers and wise men and women.

These are some of the less obvious ones:

Eye of newt - mustard seed
Toe of frog = Buttercup (Ranunculus acris L.)
Wool of bat = Holly Leaves (Ilex aquifolium)
Tongue of dog = Gypsyflower from the Genus Hound's Tounge (Cynoglossum officinale L.)
Adders fork = Least Adder's-tongue (Ophioglossum lusitanicum L.)
Blind-worm = Slowworm (Anguis fragilis)
Fillet of a fenny snake = possibly an eel or possibly plant - Indian turnip found in boggy areas.

Monday 30

Sunrise 07.00
Sunset 18.39
Moonrise 04.14
Moonset 18.07

Tuesday 1

Sunrise 07.01
Sunset 18.37
Moonrise 05.25
Moonset 18.17

Wednesday 2

Sunrise 07.03
Sunset 18.34
Moonrise 06.34
Moonset 18.26

New Moon 19.49

Thursday 3

Sunrise 07.05
Sunset 18.32
Moonrise 07.44
Moonset 18.36

Friday 4

Sunrise 07.06
Sunset 18.30
Moonrise 08.55
Moonset 18.47

Saturday 5

Sunrise 07.08
Sunset 18.28
Moonrise 10.08
Moonset 19.00

Sunday 6

Sunrise 07.10
Sunset 18.25
Moonrise 11.23
Moonset 19.19

Snails

Weather Lore: The Victorian collector of weather folklore, Richard Inwards, noted that *"It was widely believed that when there was an abundance of snails, rain was due"*. This seems obvious to us now, as snails tend to hide away in dry or very cold conditions and will not come out to feed.

He also recorded that *"Black snails on the road or path signify rain for the next day"*. Similarly, *"If snails crawl up an evergreen tree and remain there all day, wet weather is on its way."* Other observations he made include *"If a snail shoots out its horn or tentacles, the weather will be fine and sunny."*

Historic reference: To the ancient Greeks, a snail's hardworking endeavours were to be admired. To the Christians they symbolized laziness and, in Britain during the Middle Ages, this perception was turned into an insult.

Culinary: In Swindon, during the 19th century, snails were believed to be a popular health food. In the December 1984 issue of 'Wiltshire Notes and Queries' it was noted "In the neighbourhood of Swindon, it was common thing to see men snail hunting in the roadsides, filling sacks with the dainty mollusc, for which they find a ready market in the town, where snails were regarded as a delicacy."

Monday 7

Sunrise 07.11
Sunset 18.23
Moonrise 12.38
Moonset 19.45

Tuesday 8

Sunrise 07.13
Sunset 18.21
Moonrise 13.49
Moonset 20.22

Wednesday 9

Sunrise 07.15
Sunset 18.19
Moonrise 14.51
Moonset 21.16

Thursday 10

Sunrise 07.16
Sunset 18.17
Moonrise 15.38
Moonset 22.25

First Quarter 19.55

Friday 11

Sunrise 07.18
Sunset 18.14
Moonrise 16.13
Moonset 23.47

Saturday 12

Sunrise 07.20
Sunset 18.12
Moonrise 16.37
Moonset -- --

Sunday 13

Sunrise 07.21
Sunset 18.10
Moonset 01.16
Moonrise 16.55

As we move to the darker half of the year, celebrations traditionally look towards our ancestors. The image above is a sculpture at Poles Coppice in South Shropshire, made as part of the community project 'Impressions of the Past'. The sculpture looks towards and reflects the Iron Age hillfort on Earls Hill and celebrates the locality's Iron Age heritage.

Whether we collect old photographs or artifacts, or perhaps make symbols of the past we can relate to, we can all, in some small way, remember our ancestors.

Monday 14
Sunrise 07.23
Sunset 18.08
Moonset 02.46
Moonrise 17.10

Tuesday 15
Sunrise 07.25
Sunset 18.06
Moonset 04.16
Moonrise 17.23

Wednesday 16
Sunrise 07.26
Sunset 18.04
Moonset 05.47
Moonrise 17.36

Thursday 17
Sunrise 07.28
Sunset 18.02
Moonset 07.20
Moonrise 17.51

'Hunters' Moon 12.26

Friday 18
Sunrise 07.30
Sunset 17.59
Moonset 08.55
Moonrise 18.08

Saturday 19
Sunrise 07.32
Sunset 17.57
Moonset 10.30
Moonrise 18.32

Sunday 20
Sunrise 07.33
Sunset 17.55
Moonset 12.02
Moonrise 19.06

Binsey Treacle Well

The 'treacle' from Binsey Treacle Well is not what we would think of as treacle today. During medieval times the word 'triacle' or 'treacle' denoted a healing or medicinal liquid. The addition of honey (a known cure-all) made a sugary syrup or balm and over time the word treacle became to be used for any sugary liquid.

The Treacle Well in Binsey, Oxfordshire was known as a source for healing waters, thanks to Saint Frideswide. In the eighth century, the Mercian King, Ælfgar, was struck blind whilst lustfully chasing Frideswide. However, Frideswide felt sorry for the king and prayed to Saint Margaret to make the nearby waters heal him. Her prayers were answered, and the waters became known for their healing properties The well achieved later notoriety by being the 'Treacle Well' described in Lewis Caroll's book Alice in Wonderland.

Oxford students would send 'freshers' to the nearby algae-covered pool, in Binsey, telling them the waters tasted like golden syrup!

The word treacle was also attributed to mines. Treacle Mines are shrouded in mystery as to what they really are and can be found in Wem, Shropshire, Pudsey near Leeds amongst many other sites. One of the earliest stories about Treacle Mining involved billeted troops heading for Crimean War in 1853. When the troops decamped from Chobham Common, Surrey, rather than move their barrels of supplies they simply buried them, some of which contained treacle. Later, the locals on digging up the barrels found treacle and became known as 'treacle miners'!

October   Autumn

Monday 21
Sunrise 07.35
Sunset 17.53
Moonset 13.21
Moonrise 19.55

Tuesday 22
Sunrise 07.27
Sunset 17.51
Moonset 14.22
Moonrise 20.59

Wednesday 23
Sunrise 07.38
Sunset 17.49
Moonset 15.03
Moonrise 22.14

Thursday 24
Sunrise 07.40
Sunset 17.47
Moonset 15.32
Moonrise 23.32

Third Quarter 09.03

Friday 25
Sunrise 07.42
Sunset 17.45
Moonset 15.51
Moonrise -- --

Saturday 26
Sunrise 07.44
Sunset 17.43
Moonrise 00.49
Moonset 16.05

Put clocks back one hour tonight

Sunday 27
Sunrise 06.45
Sunset 16.40
Moonrise 01.03
Moonset 15.16

British Summer Time ends

The Sad Tale of Betty Corrigall

Betty Corrigall was a young woman who lived on the Orkney island of Hoy in the 18th century. During the 1770s she fell pregnant, but the father of the child abandoned her and fled to sea. Faced with shame and ruin, she took her own life. At first, she tried to drown herself, but she was rescued; then days later she succeeded by hanging herself.

Because she had committed suicide, Betty could not be buried within the kirkyard, so she was interred her in an unmarked grave on the boundary between the parishes of Hoy and North Walls.

There she lay undisturbed until 1933, when two locals, who had been digging for peat, uncovered the corner of her coffin. Believing they may have found some treasure, they opened the casket, only to discover Betty's body, along with the noose; both had been perfectly preserved in the peat bog.

Betty was reburied in the same unmarked spot and there she would have remained, but for the outbreak of the Second World War, when Hoy became home to thousands of armed forces. One day, a working party came across Betty's grave and this led to her body, which they regarded as a curio, being exhumed and reburied many times, causing it to decay. Eventually, officers covered the grave with concrete to avoid any further disturbance.

It was not until 1949 that a visiting American minister placed a wooden cross on the spot. He also asked a local official to erect a headstone; this was finally completed in 1976, when a brief service was also held for Betty.

Monday 28

Sunrise 06.47
Sunset 16.40
Moonrise 02.14
Moonset 15.26

Tuesday 29

Sunrise 06.49
Sunset 16.38
Moonrise 03.24
Moonset 15.35

Wednesday 30

Sunrise 06.51
Sunset 16.36
Moonrise 04.33
Moonset 15.45

Thursday 31

Sunrise 06.52
Sunset 16.34
Moonrise 05.44
Moonset 15.55

Samhain / All Hallows' Eve

Friday 1

Sunrise 06.54
Sunset 16.32
Moonrise 06.56
Moonset 16.08

New Moon 12.47 / All Saints' Day

Saturday 2

Sunrise 06.56
Sunset 16.30
Moonrise 08.11
Moonset 16.25

All Souls' Day

Sunday 3

Sunrise 06.58
Sunset 16.29
Moonrise 09.27
Moonset 16.49

Samhain

Some scholars believe the Irish were the first Western European people to develop full-scale vernacular written literature that expressed a range of literary genres. This 9th Century poem by an unknown author is believed to celebrate Samhain, one of the four Gaelic seasonal festivals, along with Imbolc, Beltane and Lughnasadh. It is the time when summer has passed and we enter the darker half of the year. Samhain is also known to have been observed throughout Scotland and the Isle of Man (where it is spelt Sauin). In Wales, a similar festival was kept, called Calan Gaeaf, and in Cornwall where it was known as Kalan Gway.

"I have news for you:
The stag bells, winter snows, summer has gone
wind, high and cold, the sun low, short on his course
The sea running high.
Deep red the bracken, its shape lost;
The wild geese cry,
cold grips the bird's wings;
season of ice,
this is my news."

Many people today still celebrate this time of the year in ways our ancestors may have recognised but for many it transmuted into Halloween, which developed its own popular cultural traditions, superstitions and celebrations.

November Autumn

Monday 4
Sunrise 07.00
Sunset 16.27
Moonrise 10.40
Moonset 17.23

Tuesday 5
Sunrise 07.01
Sunset 16.25
Moonrise 11.45
Moonset 18.11

Guy Fawkes Night

Wednesday 6
Sunrise 07.03
Sunset 16.24
Moonrise 12.36
Moonset 19.15

Thursday 7
Sunrise 07.05
Sunset 16.22
Moonrise 13.14
Moonset 20.32

Friday 8
Sunrise 07.07
Sunset 16.20
Moonrise 13.41
Moonset 21.56

Saturday 9
Sunrise 07.08
Sunset 16.19
Moonrise 14.00
Moonset 23.22

First Quarter 05.55

Sunday 10
Sunrise 07.10
Sunset 16.17
Moonrise 14.15
Moonset -- --

Remembrance Sunday

"Conkers, the seed of the Horse Chestnut can be used to keep spiders out of the home if strung up on thresholds or placed in windows."

"To see several foxes together is unlucky but to see a lone fox means good luck will attend you." Wales

"When the moon is full, mushrooms you may safely pull. But when the moon is on the wane, wait 'ere you think to pluck again."

Monday 11

Sunrise 07.12
Sunset 16.16
Moonset 00.49
Moonrise 14.29

Martinmas / Armistice Day

Tuesday 12

Sunrise 07.14
Sunset 16.14
Moonset 02.16
Moonrise 14.41

Wednesday 13

Sunrise 07.15
Sunset 16.13
Moonset 03.44
Moonrise 14.54

Thursday 14

Sunrise 07.17
Sunset 16.11
Moonset 05.16
Moonrise 15.10

Friday 15

Sunrise 07.19
Sunset 16.10
Moonset 06.50
Moonrise 15.30

'Moon Before Yule' 21.28

Saturday 16

Sunrise 07.20
Sunset 16.09
Moonset 08.25
Moonrise 15.59

Sunday 17

Sunrise 07.22
Sunset 16.07
Moonset 09.53
Moonrise 16.41

November Dark Skies

We are now in the darker part of the year, the perfect time for stargazing. Visible in the night sky in November are The Taurids, a long-running minor meteor shower producing only about 5-10 meteors per hour, that peak on the 4th and 5th. They are unusual in that they consist of two separate streams. Later in the month is The Leonids meteor shower that peaks on the 17th and 18th, producing up to 15 meteors per hour.

In folklore, stars have many superstitions associated with them. It was believed that *"Falling, or shooting stars are souls coming down from heaven to animate newborn children."* and *"When a death occurs the flame of life lights up a new star."* (Yorkshire)

There is an old Irish story of a woman who dreams that a spark from a falling star falls into her mouth and it was the soul of her unborn child entering her body. In Wales, it is believed that *"You must express a wish when a star shoots over you, or you will be unlucky all year."*

We use phrases such as *"Written in the stars"* and *"If the stars align"* which are both positive affirmations meaning things are meant to happen, or will happen if the circumstances prove right. They align with a belief in a 'greater power' or that fate controls our destiny.

"Twinkle, twinkle, little star,
How I wonder what you are!
Up above the world so high,
Like a diamond in the sky.

In the dark blue sky you keep,
And often thro' my curtains peep,
For you never shut your eye,
Till the sun is in the sky.

When the blazing sun is gone,
When he nothing shines upon,
Then you show your little light,
Twinkle, twinkle, all the night.

'Tis your bright and tiny spark,
Lights the trav'ller in the dark,
Tho' I know not what you are,
Twinkle, twinkle, little star".

Then the trav'ller in the dark,
Thanks you for your tiny spark,
He could not see which way to go,
If you did not twinkle so.

The poem, which is in couplet form, was first published in 1806 in Rhymes for the Nursery, a collection of poems by Jane Taylor.

Monday 18
Sunrise 07.24
Sunset 16.06
Moonset 11.05
Moonrise 17.40

Tuesday 19
Sunrise 07.24
Sunset 16.05
Moonset 11.57
Moonrise 18.53

Wednesday 20
Sunrise 07.27
Sunset 16.04
Moonset 12.31
Moonrise 20.13

Thursday 21
Sunrise 07.29
Sunset 16.03
Moonset 12.55
Moonrise 21.32

Friday 22
Sunrise 07.30
Sunset 16.02
Moonset 13.11
Moonrise 22.49

Saturday 23
Sunrise 07.32
Sunset 16.01
Moonset 13.24
Moonrise -- --

Third Quarter 01.27

Sunday 24
Sunrise 07.34
Sunset 16.00
Moonrise 00.01
Moonset 13.34

Stir Up Sunday

Winter Warmer

'A Good Huswifes Handmaide for the Kitchin' cookbook published in 1594 gives a recipe for Buttered Beere, a type of caudle, that would be a wonderful winter warmer due to its sustaining nature and is not that dissimilar to our seasonal Eggnog.

"Take three pintes of Beere, put fiue yolkes of Egges to it, straine them together, and set it in a pewter pot to the fyre, and put to it halfe a pound of Sugar, one penniworth of Nutmegs beaten, one penniworth of Cloues beaten, and a halfepenniworth of Ginger beaten, and when it is all in, take another pewter pot and brewe them together, and set it to the fire againe, and when it is readie to boyle, take it from the fire, and put a dish of sweet butter into it, and brewe them together out of one pot into an other."

Here is a translated, modernised version of the recipe to try.

Ingredients: 1½ litres of a good quality ale, 200g Demerara sugar, 5 egg yolks, 100g unsalted butter, chopped into small pieces, ½tsp ground cloves, ½tsp ground nutmeg, ¼tsp ground ginger.

Method: Pour the ale gently into a large saucepan and stir in the ginger, cloves and nutmeg. Bring slowly to the boil, then reduce the heat and simmer for a few minutes until the ale clears. While the ale is simmering, whisk the egg yolks and sugar in a bowl until the mixture is light and creamy. Remove the spiced ale from the hob, add the egg yolk and sugar mixture, and stir until all ingredients are well blended. Return to a low heat until the liquid starts to thicken, taking care not to overheat. Simmer for five minutes, then add the chopped butter and heat until it has melted. Hand-whisk the liquid until it becomes frothy. Continue to heat for 10 minutes, then allow to cool to a drinkable temperature. Give the mixture another whisk, serve in a jug or small glasses (or tankards!) and drink while still warm.

Monday 25
Sunrise 07.35
Sunset 15.59
Moonrise 01.12
Moonset 13.44

Tuesday 26
Sunrise 07.37
Sunset 15.58
Moonrise 02.21
Moonset 13.53

Wednesday 27
Sunrise 07.38
Sunset 15.57
Moonrise 03.31
Moonset 14.03

Thursday 28
Sunrise 07.40
Sunset 15.56
Moonrise 04.42
Moonset 14.15

Friday 29
Sunrise 07.41
Sunset 15.55
Moonrise 05.57
Moonset 14.31

Saturday 30
Sunrise 07.42
Sunset 15.55
Moonrise 07.13
Moonset 14.53

St. Andrew's Day (Patron Saint of Scotland)

Sunday 1
Sunrise 07.44
Sunset 15.54
Moonrise 08.28
Moonset 15.23

New Moon 06.21 / First Sunday of Advent

The Magick of Wreath Making

The tradition of making circlets of greenery and flowers goes way back, with mention of the Romans and Greeks making them to adorn themselves and their homes. It has become a well-known tradition at Yuletide to have a wreath of festive greenery to decorate the front door and the table and to take to loved ones' graves. The whole process of making a wreath and choosing the items for it can be a magickal one. The word *"wreath"* originates from the Old English word *"writhen"*, meaning *"to twist"*, so you need to start with twisting suitable bendy twigs of dogwood, willow or hazel whips. If your twigs are snapping, soak them in water overnight to make them more supple. The base circlet you make is said to represent eternal life, the continuing passage of time and a barrier against evil. The greenery you twist and tie in, of holly and ivy, is also believed to protect against malign spirits and spells. Then you can add embellishments such as cinnamon sticks, to signify abundance, pine cones to signify rebirth, mistletoe the-all-healing plant - to bring health and good luck, crab apples to represent love, and dried orange slices or whole dried oranges for prosperity.

If you want to, you can weave an intention into your wreath as you make it, by focusing on words or images which represent the qualities you want your wreath to exude throughout the festive season.

December   Autumn

Monday 2
Sunrise 07.45
Sunset 15.54
Moonrise 09.36
Moonset 16.07

Bank Holiday in Scotland

Tuesday 3
Sunrise 07.47
Sunset 15.53
Moonrise 10.33
Moonset 17.08

Wednesday 4
Sunrise 07.48
Sunset 15.53
Moonrise 11.15
Moonset 18.22

Thursday 5
Sunrise 07.49
Sunset 15.52
Moonrise 11.44
Moonset 19.44

Friday 6
Sunrise 07.50
Sunset 15.52
Moonrise 12.06
Moonset 21.09

Saturday 7
Sunrise 07.52
Sunset 15.52
Moonrise 12.22
Moonset 22.34

Sunday 8
Sunrise 07.53
Sunset 15.51
Moonrise 12.35
Moonset 23.58

First Quarter 15.26

Making wreaths from evergreens and hedgerow plants, which were simply twisted together to form a circle is an old tradition. The word "wreath" comes from the "writhen", an old English word meaning "to writhe" or "to twist." The Robins in this image have collected natural material from the hedgerow to make a wreath to celebrate Yuletide.

Monday 9
Sunrise 07.54
Sunset 15.51
Moonrise 12.47
Moonset -- --

Tuesday 10
Sunrise 07.55
Sunset 15.51
Moonset 01.22
Moonrise 13.00

Wednesday 11
Sunrise 07.56
Sunset 15.51
Moonset 02.49
Moonrise 13.14

Thursday 12
Sunrise 07.57
Sunset 15.51
Moonset 04.19
Moonrise 13.31

Friday 13
Sunrise 07.58
Sunset 15.51
Moonset 05.51
Moonrise 13.55

Saturday 14
Sunrise 07.59
Sunset 15.51
Moonset 07.22
Moonrise 14.30

Sunday 15
Sunrise 08.00
Sunset 15.51
Moonset 08.42
Moonrise 15.20

'Oak' Moon 09.01

December

"On Christmas day ,when fires were lit,
And all our breakfasts done, We spread our toys out on the floor
And played there in the sun.
The nursery smelled of Christmas tree,
And under where it stood
The shepherds watched their flocks of sheep,
All made of painted wood.
Outside the house the air was cold
And quiet all about,
Till far across the snowy roofs
The Christmas bells rang out.
But soon the sleigh-bells jingled by
Upon the street below,
And people on the way to church,.
Went crunching through the snow
We did not Quarrel once all day;
Mamma and Grandma said
They liked to be in where we were,
So pleasantly we played.
I do not see how any child
Is cross on Christmas Day ,
When all the lovely toys are new,
And everyone can play."
Vintage poem by K Pyle

December   Autumn

Monday 16
Sunrise 08.00
Sunset 15.51
Moonset 09.44
Moonrise 16.28

Tuesday 17
Sunrise 08.01
Sunset 15.52
Moonset 10.26
Moonrise 17.47

Wednesday 18
Sunrise 08.02
Sunset 15.52
Moonset 10.55
Moonrise 19.09

Thursday 19
Sunrise 08.02
Sunset 15.52
Moonset 11.15
Moonrise 20.29

Friday 20
Sunrise 08.03
Sunset 15.53
Moonset 11.29
Moonrise 21.44

Saturday 21
Sunrise 08.03
Sunset 15.53
Moonset 11.40
Moonrise 22.56

Yule/Winter Solstice 09.19/Midwinter's Day/Winter officially begins

Sunday 22
Sunrise 08.04
Sunset 15.54
Moonset 11.50
Moonrise -- --

Third Quarter 22.18

A Recipe for the Season

Charles Dickens has become synonymous with the festive season and the blueprint for seasonal festivities is often attributed to his novel, 'A Christmas Carol'. Dickens' eldest daughter, Mamie, recounted her family's 'eagerness and delight' with which they looked forward to Christmas and described her father creating magic lanterns for the children, doing conjuring tricks, dressing as a magician and making the children scream with laughter.

In 'A Christmas Carol' we are told that Bob Cratchit drinks a punch made of gin and lemon, which is thought to refer to the then-popular Gin Twist. This was made by putting gin, sugar syrup, lemon juice and a twist of peel in a mug, then heating it up by inserting a hot poker from the fire.

A popular parlour game of this time, particularly recommended to add

to the seasonal mirth, was 'Bullet Pudding'. This consisted of a compressed mound of flour with a grape on top and the players would each, in turn, slice away at the flour until the grape was toppled. Whoever toppled the grape had to pick it up by mouth, so the winning player was likely to become covered in flour.

Add to the mix festive greenery, a plum pudding and, of course, a good measure of ghost stories!

Monday 23

Sunrise 08.04
Sunset 15.54
Moonrise 00.07
Moonset 12.00

Tuesday 24

Sunrise 08.05
Sunset 15.55
Moonrise 01.16
Moonset 12.10

Advent ends / Christmas Eve

Wednesday 25

Sunrise 08.05
Sunset 15.56
Moonrise 02.27
Moonset 12.21

Christmas Day (Quarter Day)

Thursday 26

Sunrise 08.05
Sunset 15.56
Moonrise 03.40
Moonset 12.35

Boxing Day

Friday 27

Sunrise 08.05
Sunset 15.57
Moonrise 04.55
Moonset 12.54

Saturday 28

Sunrise 08.06
Sunset 15.58
Moonrise 06.11
Moonset 13.21

Sunday 29

Sunrise 08.06
Sunset 15.59
Moonrise 07.23
Moonset 14.00

Winter Solstice

Quite how long people have celebrated the Winter Solstice, or midwinter, in this country is not known; much is alluded to but there is little fact. But over 5,000 years ago, Stone Age farmers built Newgrange passage tomb in what is now County Meath in Ireland. This structure was built to align with the morning sun during the solstice period, creating a shaft of light that illuminates a spiral motif on the back stone slab in the chamber. Stonehenge too is believed to have been 'designed' around the celestial sky of the Winter Solstice. Many ancient sites may also lay claim to having been built for this time of the year, when our sun, even at its weakest, can fill us with awe.

Certainly, the Anglo Saxons went wassailing in winter, a custom rooted in an older pagan magic. Singing, feasting and merriment took place as they encouraged nature to favour a good harvest in the coming year. Winter was the time of no farming, little trading and little work and was a generally miserable time. What better way to raise the spirits than to make merry wassailing? The 'rebirth of the sun' was welcomed as the light was literally coming back into people's lives.

It is no coincidence that this time was chosen by the Christian church to celebrate 'the birth of the son of God' and so traditions and beliefs gradually mixed together, resulting in this time when we have Yuletide celebrations that encompass our need to mark midwinter and also bring light and hope into our lives.

For us personally, marking these significant times in our year and acknowledging the seasons is about connecting with nature and spending time with her, celebrating the light and dark aspects of this season.

December   Winter

Monday 30
Sunrise 08.06
Sunset 16.00
Moonrise 08.25
Moonset 14.56

New Moon 02.26

Tuesday 31
Sunrise 08.06
Sunset 16.01
Moonrise 09.13
Moonset 16.07

New Year's Eve

Wednesday 1
Sunrise 08.06
Sunset 16.02
Moonrise 09.47
Moonset 17.29

New Year's Day

Thursday 2
Sunrise 08.05
Sunset 16.03
Moonrise 10.11
Moonset 18.55

Friday 3
Sunrise 08.05
Sunset 16.04
Moonrise 10.28
Moonset 20.22

Saturday 4
Sunrise 08.05
Sunset 16.05
Moonrise 10.42
Moonset 21.46

Sunday 5
Sunrise 08.05
Sunset 16.07
Moonrise 10.55
Moonset 23.10

Winter

The word 'winter' is of Old English and is thought to refer to the word for wet. Astronomically, winter occurs from the winter solstice to the vernal equinox.

"Oh winter, ruler of th' inverted year,
Thy scatter'd hair with sleet like ashes fill'd,
Thy breath congeal'd upon thy lips, thy cheeks
Fring'd with a beard made white with other snows
Than those of age, thy forehead wrapp'd in clouds,
A leafless branch thy sceptre, and thy throne
A sliding car, indebted to no wheels,
But urg'd by storms along its slipp'ry way,
I love thee, all unlovely as thou seem'st,
And dreaded as thou art! Thou hold'st the sun
A pris'ner in the yet undawning east,
Short'ning his journey between morn and noon,
And hurrying him, impatient of his stay,
Down to the rosy west; but kindly still
Compensating his loss with added hours
Of social converse and instructive ease,
And gath'ring, at short notice, in one group
The family dispers'd, and fixing thought,
Not less dispers'd by day-light and its cares.
I crown thee king of intimate delights,
Fire-side enjoyments, home-born happiness,
And all the comforts that the lowly roof
Of undisturb'd retirement, and the hours
Of long uninterrupted ev'ning, know."
William Cowper - (1731-1800)

Monday 6
Sunrise 08.04
Sunset 16.08
Moonrise 11.07
Moonset -- --

First Quarter 23.56

Tuesday 7
Sunrise 08.04
Sunset 16.09
Moonset 00.35
Moonrise 11.20

Wednesday 8
Sunrise 08.03
Sunset 16.10
Moonset 02.01
Moonrise 11.35

Thursday 9
Sunrise 08.03
Sunset 16.12
Moonset 03.30
Moonrise 11.56

Friday 10
Sunrise 08.02
Sunset 16.13
Moonset 04.59
Moonrise 12.25

Saturday 11
Sunrise 08.02
Sunset 16.15
Moonset 06.22
Moonrise 13.07

Sunday 12
Sunrise 08.01
Sunset 16.16
Moonset 07.30
Moonrise 14.07

As we say farewell to 2024, we immediately find ourselves with a new year full of calendar customs, traditions and nature observations to celebrate in our seasonal cycle. Our 'Goldilocks-Planet' on which live is close enough to the Sun to allow us liquid water and is neither too hot nor too cold to sustain life; with a tilt that gives us seasonal variances and a moon of the correct distance, size and alignment to give us tides and eclipses, is truly something to wonder at and be thankful for.

Whilst we are indeed struggling to address the damage we have caused to our home planet, Earth, there is cause for hope, as many people are showing that they care enough to be actively involved in halting and attempting to reverse it. As always Mother Nature 'brings us down to earth' if we take the trouble to notice as she guides and helps us through. At a time when all seems barren and lifeless, even in Winter, the emergence of the tiny, hope-giving snowdrops together with other signs of new life such as catkins and resident and over-wintering birds busy on feeding stations, we are reminded that as something comes to an end something else will begin.

At Talking Trees, we too follow this wonderful magickal cycle when creating our publications, cards and posters. This enables us to connect you with special times throughout the year as we try to keep alive the old ways and celebrate the new. We are so thankful for your interest and your companionship each year.

Notes

2025

JANUARY
Su	Mo	Tu	We	Th	Fr	Sa
			1	2	3	4
5	6	7	8	9	10	11
12	13	14	15	16	17	18
19	20	21	22	23	24	25
26	27	28	29	30	31	

FEBRUARY
Su	Mo	Tu	We	Th	Fr	Sa
						1
2	3	4	5	6	7	8
9	10	11	12	13	14	15
16	17	18	19	20	21	22
23	24	25	26	27	28	

MARCH
Su	Mo	Tu	We	Th	Fr	Sa
						1
2	3	4	5	6	7	8
9	10	11	12	13	14	15
16	17	18	19	20	21	22
23	24	25	26	27	28	29
30	31					

APRIL
Su	Mo	Tu	We	Th	Fr	Sa
		1	2	3	4	5
6	7	8	9	10	11	12
13	14	15	16	17	18	19
20	21	22	23	24	25	26
27	28	29	30			

MAY
Su	Mo	Tu	We	Th	Fr	Sa
				1	2	3
4	5	6	7	8	9	10
11	12	13	14	15	16	17
18	19	20	21	22	23	24
25	26	27	28	29	30	31

JUNE
Su	Mo	Tu	We	Th	Fr	Sa
1	2	3	4	5	6	7
8	9	10	11	12	13	14
15	16	17	18	19	20	21
22	23	24	25	26	27	28
29	30					

JULY
Su	Mo	Tu	We	Th	Fr	Sa
		1	2	3	4	5
6	7	8	9	10	11	12
13	14	15	16	17	18	19
20	21	22	23	24	25	26
27	28	29	30	31		

AUGUST
Su	Mo	Tu	We	Th	Fr	Sa
					1	2
3	4	5	6	7	8	9
10	11	12	13	14	15	16
17	18	19	20	21	22	23
24	25	26	27	28	29	30
31						

SEPTEMBER
Su	Mo	Tu	We	Th	Fr	Sa
	1	2	3	4	5	6
7	8	9	10	11	12	13
14	15	16	17	18	19	20
21	22	23	24	25	26	27
28	29	30				

OCTOBER
Su	Mo	Tu	We	Th	Fr	Sa
			1	2	3	4
5	6	7	8	9	10	11
12	13	14	15	16	17	18
19	20	21	22	23	24	25
26	27	28	29	30	31	

NOVEMBER
Su	Mo	Tu	We	Th	Fr	Sa
						1
2	3	4	5	6	7	8
9	10	11	12	13	14	15
16	17	18	19	20	21	22
23	24	25	26	27	28	29
30						

DECEMBER
Su	Mo	Tu	We	Th	Fr	Sa
	1	2	3	4	5	6
7	8	9	10	11	12	13
14	15	16	17	18	19	20
21	22	23	24	25	26	27
28	29	30	31			

To purchase greeting cards of images from our diaries or any of our other endeavours, please scan the QR code.

or visit
www.talkingtreesbooks.co.uk

or our Etsy shop at

etsy.com/uk/shop/TalkingTreeBooksCo?ele=shop_open

Printed in Great Britain
by Amazon

37796645R00066